This Book Comes With a Website

Nolo's award-winning website has a page dedicated just to this book, where you can:

DOWNLOAD FORMS – All the forms and worksheets in the book are accessible online

KEEP UP TO DATE – When there are important changes to the information in this book, we'll post updates

READ BLOGS – Get the latest info from Nolo authors' blogs

LISTEN TO PODCASTS – Listen to authors discuss timely issues on topics that interest you

WATCH VIDEOS – Get a quick introduction to a legal topic with our short videos

You'll find the link in the appendix.

And that's not all. Nolo.com contains thousands of articles on everyday legal and business issues, plus a plain-English law dictionary, all written by Nolo experts and available for free. You'll also find more useful **books, software, online services,** and **downloadable forms.**

Get forms and more at
www.nolo.com

DOWNLOAD FORMS

at nolo.com

Smart Policies for Workplace Technologies

Email, Blogs, Cell Phones & More

Lisa Guerin, J.D.

THIRD EDITION	JANUARY 2013
Editor	RICHARD STIM
Cover Design	JALEH DOANE
Proofreading	NICOLE THOMAS
Index	JULIE SHAWVAN
Printing	BANG PRINTING

Guerin, Lisa, 1964-
  Smart policies for workplace technologies : email, blogs, cell phones & more / Lisa Guerin. -- 3rd ed.
    p. cm.
  ISBN 978-1-4133-1843-2 (pbk.) -- ISBN 978-1-4133-1844-9 (epub ebook)
1. Personal Internet use in the workplace. 2. Business enterprises--Computer networks--Security measures. 3. Telecommunication. 4. Blogs. 5. Personnel management. 6. Labor laws and legislation--United States. I. Title.
  HF5549.5.P39G84 2013
  651.7--dc23

                            2012035338

This book covers only United States law, unless it specifically states otherwise.

Please note

We believe accurate, plain-English legal information should help you solve many of your own legal problems. But this text is not a substitute for personalized advice from a knowledgeable lawyer. If you want the help of a trained professional—and we'll always point out situations in which we think that's a good idea—consult an attorney licensed to practice in your state.

About the Author

Lisa Guerin is an editor at Nolo specializing in employment law. She is the author or coauthor of several Nolo books, including *The Manager's Legal Handbook*, *Dealing With Problem Employees*, *The Essential Guide to Federal Employment Laws*, *The Essential Guide to Workplace Investigations*, *Create Your Own Employee Handbook*, *The Essential Guide to Family and Medical Leave*, *The Progressive Discipline Handbook*, and *Nolo's Guide to California Law*. Ms. Guerin has practiced employment law in government, public interest, and private practice, where she represented clients at all levels of state and federal courts and in agency proceedings. She is a graduate of Boalt Hall School of Law at the University of California at Berkeley.

Table of Contents

Appendix

Index

Drafting Effective Technology Policies

n the not-so-distant past, every telephone had a cord tethering the caller to a nearby wall. The only way a business could transmit a document was to place it an envelope and pay someone to carry it to the recipient. To research important data, we had to find the right books, sometimes by traveling to a library, then take them off the shelf, open them, and hope that the table of contents would point us to the relevant pages.

For anyone under 20 years old, these must some seem like some outdated and inefficient limitations for operating a business. Nowadays, smartphones, email, the Internet, cloud computing, and other innovations have brought huge gains in business efficiency and productivity, allowing instant communication and access to information that would have seemed unimaginable only a short time ago.

And, of course, the technology wave hasn't crested yet. Every time we turn around, there's a new device—or an innovative way to use something we've already got—that could revolutionize the way we work. One day, not too long from now, we'll look back on iPhones, Twitter, and spam with the same nostalgia we reserve for the inkwell, carbon paper, and the IBM Selectric.

But no matter how technology evolves, one thing remains constant: New technology always brings new risks for employers. Technology can always be misused, either intentionally or accidentally. And, because employers are often legally responsible for the acts of their employees, technological developments have exponentially increased the possibility of legal exposure.

In recent years, we've been inundated with tales of employer woes: private customer information accidentally made public; racist or sexist jokes transmitted through a company's email system; employees causing car accidents while doing business on their cell phones; blogs that reveal company trade secrets; employees or officers "outed" as the authors of glowing online reviews of company products; and employees airing workplace gripes on social networking sites. Although technology has promised to increase efficiency and rid us of documentation, it sometimes seems to have had the opposite effect—for example, companies now spend thousands of dollars combing through their electronic files to produce evidence for auditors, courts, and government agencies.

How does an employer modulate this digital din? Some try to control technology with other technology—for example, software that blocks certain Internet sites, programs that scan email for illegal content, or company-wide adoption of digital passwords to prevent access to company secrets. But fighting technology with technology is a never-ending game of cat and mouse, as the makers of anti-spam software have learned. There's always a way to skirt these technological solutions, which means companies have to develop a response to the workaround, and the escalation continues.

Ten Ways Around Your Company's Technological Controls

Many companies, especially those with a savvy IT department, rely on blocking software, filters, and other technology to prevent employees from wasting resources or compromising security by, for example, surfing porn sites, sending large files, or storing work-related documents online. If the employees are also tech-savvy, however, they can get around these controls—and they often want to, because it's easier and more convenient. Often, these employees aren't troublemakers; they're just trying to work from home, get the programs or files they need, or save more email messages than your company's system allows.

This is one reason why your company must not only physically block employees from misusing company technology, but also adopt a policy prohibiting it and explaining why it's important. Employees who know the risks of getting around the company's controls are more likely to think twice before taking that shortcut. And if you're thinking your company's employees probably don't know the first thing about circumventing the company's controls, you better hope they don't read *The Wall Street Journal*, which published a list of ten controls and how to get around them. It explains how to:

- **Send large files:** Use an online service to transmit large files free.

Ten Ways Around Your Company's Technological Controls (continued)

- **Use software the company doesn't allow employees to download:** Access a Web-based version of the software or load it on a portable device.
- **Visit blocked websites:** Use a proxy site to see the blocked website rather than visiting it directly, either through a search or by asking Google to do an English-to-English translation of the site (which calls it up on the searcher's screen).
- **Erase tracks from a company-issued laptop:** Use the browser to delete the history of websites visited.
- **Search for work documents from home:** Store copies of files from one computer online, to be searched from another computer.
- **Store work documents online:** Use an online storage service or send files from work to a personal email account.
- **Evade company monitoring of Web-based email:** Encrypt messages or use a secure email session.
- **Access work email remotely:** Automatically forward all work-related email to a personal account.
- **Access personal email from a company-issued BlackBerry:** Add a personal email account to your profile at your BlackBerry's service provider website.
- **Avoid getting caught surfing the Web:** Hit Alt-Tab to minimize one window and maximize another.

Vauhini Vara, "Ten Things Your IT Department Won't Tell You," *The Wall Street Journal*, July 30, 2007.

A better approach is to adopt a set of commonsense rules that explain how employees should use the technologies the company makes available to them. Of course, policies alone won't stop all employee misconduct—there will always be employees who act badly, no matter what your company's handbook says. But policies, combined with training, leadership by example, and consistent enforcement, will help your company make sure that employees are using its electronic resources as the company intends.

And, if an employee doesn't follow the rules, policies provide a strong measure of legal protection if your company has to discipline or fire the employee, or prove that it did everything it could to prevent the incident (in the unfortunate event someone was harmed by an employee's misuse of technology).

This book provides policies you can adapt for your workplace on email use, employee blogs, posting to company-sponsored social media pages, using cell phones for work, downloading software, Internet access, and much more. It also provides the information you need to decide whether to use a particular policy and how to customize it to fit your workplace.

Chips and Scanners: What's Next for Workplace Tech

Most of the electronic tools covered in this book will be familiar to you. Even if you don't own a tablet or use instant messaging, you're probably familiar with these commonplace innovations. On the horizon, however, are some truly sci-fi technology applications, some of which have already been adopted in the workplace.

A lot of these innovations are intended to be used on employees, not necessarily by them. Devices once used to track packages are now being used to track people. And, developments in biometrics are being pressed into service as employee identification devices. Here are some examples:

- **Global positioning devices.** GPS devices are used not only to keep tabs on pets, children, and valuable merchandise, but also to monitor the fleets—and employees—at FedEx and United Parcel Service (UPS).
- **Radio Frequency Identification (RFID).** RFID isn't just used to identify and track people and products via a tag or transponder; it's also being used to maintain business security and track

Chips and Scanners: What's Next for Workplace Tech (continued)

employees' movements within a facility. (The RFIDs are commonly planted in employee ID badges.) At least one company has asked employees to have an RFID chip implanted in their arms to access the company's data center. These developments have led at least four states—California, North Dakota, Oklahoma, and Wisconsin—to pass laws prohibiting involuntary microchipping. (Nightclub owners have also discovered a use for RFIDs—to identify VIP customers and allow them to run a tab at the bar.) For information on state RFID laws, go to the website of the National Conference of State Legislatures, www.ncsl.org, and select the "Telecommunications/IT" issue area.

- **Biometrics.** Verifying a person's identity through their unique physical characteristics is nothing new; police departments have been using fingerprints for this purpose for decades. But some companies are now pressing this technology into use to identify employees. At McDonalds, for example, employees clock in by scanning their hands rather than punching in a time card. Some companies use facial recognition and retina scanning systems to authenticate the identity of employees entering secured areas of a facility. The federal government is even considering biometric technology to identify workers as part of the eVerify program.

Use of these technologies on employees has met with a lot of resistance, and it's no wonder why: There's a disturbing level of intrusion involved in having a chip implanted in your body or having your every move tracked. Once this information is gathered, there's also the problem of keeping it safe. Identity theft is one thing, but what about the possibility of having your facial features "hacked" and misused, or having the government subpoena records of your movements, captured through a GPS or RFID system? The legal battles over these technologies are just getting started, so stay tuned.

Why You Need Technology Policies

Your company probably has some written policies gathered in an employee handbook or policy manual, covering things like time off, benefits, employee conduct, and termination procedures. Unfortunately, however, many companies have neglected to keep up with the times by creating policies dealing with technology. Sometimes, the company's decision makers don't understand how technological innovations work or don't know how employees are actually using company resources. Sometimes, policy makers assume that existing policies are adequate to cover new technologies. Perhaps most often, however, the people responsible for writing policies just have too many other things to do, and put off updating their handbook to a later date.

> **CAUTION**
>
> **Practice makes policy.** A policy can exist without being written down or even communicated orally to employees. For example, if everyone in a company, from senior management on down, uses the company's email system for personal messages, that's company policy, even if the company has no official written guidelines saying that it's okay to use email in this way. The company would have a tough time defending a decision to fire an employee for sending personal messages if everyone else did so with impunity. It's much better to consciously decide what your company's policies should be than to create policies by default.

If your company has procrastinated on drafting or updating its technology policies, you're missing an opportunity to protect the company's assets and leaving yourselves open to legal trouble in the future. Here are some ways that well-drafted technology policies can help your company.

Protect Trade Secrets

Employees stealing trade secrets once had to stand over a copy machine, smuggle out boxes of documents, or bring in cameras.

Today, however, the valuable intangible information upon which many companies are built—their trade secrets—can easily be purloined in digital format.

Technology policies can help protect against loss of company trade secrets, whether it occurs intentionally—as when an employee steals data to sell to a competitor or start a similar business—or unintentionally—as when an employee sends confidential information through Web-based email, which is hacked by an outsider, or stores sensitive files on a smart phone that is later stolen. Even if your company faces an aggressive trade secret thief who doesn't care about the rules, strong policy language will help your company show that it took steps to protect its confidential information, which will work in your company's favor when it tries to stop others from using its stolen secrets.

Promote Your Company—Effectively and Legally

These days, consumers look for information about products and services online. Your company's official Internet presence—on its own website, in company blogs, and on the company's social media pages—plays a significant role in creating and maintaining your company's reputation. And, its "unofficial" presence—in personal blogs and posts, online reviews, or YouTube videos, for example—may be just as important, for better or for worse. Policies that draw clear lines on what employees should and shouldn't say online, whether in company-authorized content or in personal posts, can help you make sure that your company is being represented positively and appropriately in cyberspace.

Preserve Customer and Employee Privacy

All companies keep some confidential information about their employees, whether Social Security numbers, next of kin, or medical records. Many companies also have confidential customer information, such as addresses, telephone numbers, and credit card accounts. Companies have a legal obligation (and obvious

Lessons From the Real World

Technology policies help company prevent former employees from using its customer information.

Andrew Verity and Christina Chang, a married couple, worked for Creative Marketing Concepts (CMC), a San Francisco company that sold merchandise branded with corporate logos. Verity left the company after efforts to negotiate a mutually agreeable severance arrangement fell through; Chang was fired shortly after for refusing to sign a nondisclosure agreement.

Here's why CMC might have wanted that agreement: After leaving CMC, Verity and Chang started their own business and allegedly solicited CMC's customers. CMC sued Verity and Chang for trade secret theft and asked the court to issue a restraining order prohibiting the couple from using its trade secrets or soliciting its customers. The couple filed a counterclaim, suing CMC for a number of alleged wrongs stemming from the termination of their employment.

At the heart of the lawsuit were CMC's alleged trade secrets: its client list and related information, such as purchasing history, sales volume, pricing, and buying habits. The court found that this information constituted a trade secret and ordered Verity and Chang not to use it in their business. The court also dismissed Chang's claim that she was wrongfully terminated for refusing to sign the nondisclosure agreement: Because CMC had legitimate trade secrets to protect, the court found that CMC could fire her because she wouldn't sign an agreement not to disclose them.

CMC's policies were an important piece of evidence in its favor. Under California law and the Uniform Trade Secret Act, a company must show that it took reasonable steps to maintain the confidentiality of its trade secrets. CMC met this requirement by showing, among other things, that its employee handbook included rules addressing trade secret theft, including prohibitions on taking home client files and forwarding company email without authorization.

Lillge v. Verity, 2008 Westlaw 906466 (N.D. Cal. April 1, 2008); *Lillge v. Verity*, 2007 Westlaw 2900568 (N.D. Cal. Oct. 2, 2007).

incentive) to maintain the privacy of this information, which up-to-date technology policies will help you do. Many states also require companies to notify consumers if their information is leaked, stolen, or otherwise compromised.

More Than 500 Million Breached Records ... and Counting

A stolen laptop here, a hacked website there, and the security breaches start to add up. According to the Privacy Rights Clearinghouse, more than 560 million records were compromised between January 2005 and September 2012, and the number is increasing by the thousands daily. The Clearinghouse keeps an extensive database of security breaches involving consumer information (you can view it at www.privacyrights.org; select "Data Breaches" from the home page).

Lay the Groundwork for Discipline and Termination

Policies provide the basis for employee discipline and termination by explaining what conduct is prohibited. Although most companies have the right to fire employees at will (that is, for any reason that's not illegal), it's always wise, for legal and practical reasons, to fire only for good cause. By putting employees on notice, technology policies make it more difficult for employees to later argue that they were treated unfairly or that they didn't know their conduct was prohibited.

CAUTION

Policies must be enforced consistently. Having policies on paper is a good first step, but it isn't enough to protect your company from wrongful termination lawsuits. To use a policy as a lawsuit defense strategy, your company must be able to show that everyone who violated the policy faced the same consequences. Otherwise, an employee can use your company's selective enforcement as proof of discrimination, retaliation, or other unfair treatment.

Tell Employees That Their Communications Aren't Private

Because your company may one day have to read or monitor employee email messages and Internet browsing histories, you should put employees on notice. It's only fair to tell employees ahead of time that their messages may be read. Notifying employees about monitoring will also deter them from sending inappropriate messages in the first place—your ultimate goal. What's more, employees' legal right to privacy is determined, in part, by how much privacy they reasonably expect to have. If your company tells employees their communications aren't private, it will be hard for them to argue later that they nonetheless expected confidentiality.

Avoid Problems Caused by Employee Mistakes

Many of the problems created by workplace technology are the result of inadvertent errors—for example, clicking on an attachment that unleashes a virus or posting confidential information when answering a customer question online—not intentional missteps. By setting ground rules for employees and explaining why those rules are important, technology policies can help your company avoid many of these problems in the first place.

Conserve Company Resources

Misuse of technology—whether in the form of streaming audio, visiting illicit websites, or sending excessive personal email—costs time and money. Your company can preserve its bandwidth and server capacity, and maintain higher employee productivity, by adopting policies that limit how employees may use its technological resources.

Limit Liability for Employee Misconduct

In some situations, your company can use its policies to show that it tried to prevent harm to others. For example, if your company has a

Lessons From the Real World

Company can read email, even if the employee has a confidential password.

When Nissan hired Bonita Bourke to help employees with problems related to their computer system, the company probably had no idea just how much Ms. Bourke planned to use that computer.

The first sign of trouble was during a training session. In trying to demonstrate how dealership management could use email effectively, one of Ms. Bourke's coworkers pulled up a message at random to use as a teaching tool. Unfortunately for Ms. Bourke, it was a personal, sexual message that she had sent to another employee.

After the incident was reported to management, the company reviewed the entire workgroup's email messages. It found a number of personal messages, including messages with sexual overtones, sent by Ms. Bourke, who was fired.

Ms. Bourke sued Nissan for violating her privacy rights, among other things. The court ruled against her, however. Ms. Bourke had signed a form indicating her understanding that company policy restricted use of company computers to business purposes only. She also knew that email messages were occasionally read by someone other than the intended recipient. The court therefore found that, even though Ms. Bourke had a confidential password to use her computer, she could not reasonably expect her email messages to be private.

Bourke v. Nissan Motor Corp., No B068705 (California Court of Appeal, 2nd District, 1993).

written policy prohibiting employees from making business-related calls while driving, that policy can be used as evidence that the company shouldn't be legally responsible for injuries an employee caused while doing just that.

Employers' Duty to Retain and Hand Over Electronic Evidence

In 2006, federal rules took effect that define the obligations of lawsuit opponents to save and provide electronically stored evidence. The Federal Rules of Civil Procedure (FRCP), which apply to all noncriminal federal lawsuits, were updated to reflect that modern business documents are more likely to be stored on a server, disk, or backup tape—or even in the cloud—than in a filing cabinet.

The FRCP now explicitly includes electronically stored information in the categories of documents and evidence that must be exchanged in discovery: the process of requesting and receiving information from the other side and from witnesses in a lawsuit. The rules have always obligated parties to discuss the case and exchange key evidence and witness lists early on (this is called the "meet and confer" requirement). Now, electronically stored information must be discussed and produced at this meeting, which is supposed to take place only a few months after a lawsuit is filed.

The rules impose a heavy obligation on companies to properly organize their electronic information so it can be accessed and reviewed quickly for a lawsuit. However, there's some good news here for companies that routinely purge emails and electronic information: There's no penalty if a party can't provide electronic data because it was lost as a result of the routine, good faith operation of an information system. But this "safe harbor" provision applies only until litigation is in the offing. Companies facing a lawsuit must immediately stop their purging, shredding, and deleting, and impose a "litigation hold." A company that destroys potentially relevant evidence after a lawsuit is imminent can face huge fines and penalties.

Manage Electronic Documents

Most of the innovations covered in this book allow employees to create, modify, and transmit documents electronically. They also create their own electronic records, in the form of logs, user records, browsing history, address books, and so on. Employers have a duty to preserve and hand over electronic documents like these in a lawsuit, just as if they were pieces of paper. Without policies telling employees how to manage their electronic documents, your company won't be able to meet these obligations. Lawsuits aside, if employees don't know which electronic documents to keep and where to put them, your company might not be able to access important records like contracts and customer orders.

Creating Your Policies

This book will help you draft and update technology policies that will be effective in your company. What this book can't do, however, is tell you which policies are right for your company: That will depend on the industry, your corporate culture, the sophistication of your employees, your company's comfort level with risk, and plenty of other intangibles that will vary from company to company.

A large part of your job will be to decide how intrusive or trusting your company wants to be with its employees. This issue comes up again and again in the technology field because employee use of each of these devices and functions can be monitored. Here are some questions you may have to consider:

- Will your company read every employee email message or will it simply reserve its right to monitor email if it needs to?
- Will your company block access to certain Internet sites, monitor employee Internet traffic, or just tell employees not to visit certain types of sites?
- Will your company allow—or ask—employees to use personal phones and other electronic devices for work or prohibit them from doing so?

- Will your company ban all camera phones at work or ask employees not to use them in certain areas?

Each chapter in this book covers a different type of electronic resource or function, such as email, camera phones, or social media, providing an overview of the most important issues to consider, sample policy language, and information that will help your company decide whether—and how much—to regulate employee use of that equipment.

Although some policies should be adopted in every company (prohibiting employees from using cell phones while driving, for example), others are not so universal. That's why your first step in crafting technology policies is not to open this book to the appropriate chapter, but instead to figure out what your company is already doing and what it wants to do.

Determine Your Current Practices

To get started, find out how technology is being used and regulated in your company now. First, consult your company's employee handbook or other written policies. Does your company have policies in place dealing with email, blogs, cell phones, and the other equipment addressed in this book? Are these policies up to date and adequate to address all of the technology your company and its employees currently use? Does your company require employees to sign acknowledgment forms demonstrating that they have received, read, and understood these policies?

Once you've collected and reviewed your company's written policies, it's time to get out of your office and talk to people to find out what's actually happening—what types of technology are actually in use, and in what ways. Here are some ideas to help you get started:

- **Talk to your IT department** (if your company has one). Find out what technologies your company supports and what it prohibits. Does IT have the capacity to read employee email and instant messages or to track employee Internet use? Is someone actually reading employee communications? Does the company block access to certain websites? Does the company provide cell phones, smartphones, or laptops to employees? Does it allow—or require—employees to use their own electronic devices for work? If so, are there any limits on the makes or models, or on an employee's ability to access the company's network? Is IT aware of any problems in employee use or misuse of equipment?

- **Interview company managers.** What technological resources do they use in their departments? Do they issue equipment to employees? Do they encourage employees to purchase their own equipment to use for work? Are they concerned about employee use of technology? Have they had to discipline or fire any employees for misusing electronic resources? What types of equipment do they need for their departments to function most efficiently and productively?

- **Meet with the online team.** Talk to the employees who oversee your company's online presence and find out what your company is doing on the Internet. Is it active in social media channels? Does it have business blogs—and if so, how does it handle reader comments? Are you podcasting or producing online video? Does the company keep track of what others are saying about it online? The answers to these questions will help you figure out whether and how you need to address employee contributions—whether official or unofficial—to the company's online presence.

- **Consult with the lawyers.** Talk to your company's attorney to find out whether there are any special concerns—or past problems—you'll need to address. Has the company had to discipline or fire employees for electronic misconduct? Are there special concerns in your industry that you should consider? Do your state's laws or applicable court decisions address privacy and technology?

- **Get feedback from employees.** Find out what employees are really doing. Although you could talk directly to employees, you'll probably get more accurate results with an anonymous survey or questionnaire. Your goal is to find out how employees are really using the available technology, and in a face-to-face interview few employees will admit to things like sending personal email, visiting websites that aren't related to work, or getting around the company's electronic controls.

Electronic Monitoring at Work

The American Management Association (AMA) has been surveying employers about their monitoring of employee activity since 2001. The most recent survey, for 2007, reveals that many employers monitor employee email and Internet activity. Here's what they're looking at:

- **Email.** 43% of the companies surveyed monitor employee email. Almost ¾ of those use technology to automatically review messages, and 40% have an actual human being read email. Perhaps as a result of this monitoring, 28% of the companies who responded to the survey had fired someone for misuse of email, mostly in the form of inappropriate or offensive language or violation of company rules.
- **Internet use.** Of the companies surveyed, ⅔ monitor employee Internet connections, and the same number block certain sites. 30% of the companies had fired someone for Internet misuse, with the vast majority of terminations resulting from viewing, downloading, or uploading inappropriate or offensive material.
- **Computer use.** 45% of the companies track content, keystrokes, and time spent at the keyboard, and almost the same number review computer files.
- **Outside sites.** 12% of responding companies monitor blogs to find out what's being said about them, and 10% monitor social networking sites.

Draft Policies

Don't be surprised or concerned if your interviews revealed confusion about your company's current policies and expectations, or differences in the way technology is used or managed in different departments. Your job now is to use that information to come up with policies that will work for the whole company and be enforced consistently in the future.

For each type of technology your company uses, go to the appropriate chapter in this book and review the policy language provided. Some chapters include alternatives to choose from, depending on how your company wants to handle a particular issue; some also include optional language you can include if, for example, you use monitoring software or provide employees with hands-free telephone equipment. Each chapter starts with a checklist of policy provisions, so you can make sure you've considered every important issue. Most readers should be able to put together effective policies using the language provided in the book and on the CD-ROM, with very few changes.

If, however, your company requires a different approach or wants to address additional concerns, you may need to draft or modify policy language. Here are a few rules to keep in mind:

- **Keep it simple.** Use short sentences and paragraphs, and easily understood vocabulary. Be as clear and concise as possible.
- **Know your audience.** Write in the language and style that reflects the culture of your company, and the education and sophistication of its employees.
- **Explain the policy.** When writing a technology policy, it's especially important to explain the purpose behind it. Employees who don't understand why it's important not to, for example, open an unscanned email attachment, send confidential information through Web-based email, or post "anonymous" reviews of your company's products, might assume the company is just being paternalistic in imposing these requirements. Employees who know why a policy is necessary are more likely to follow it (and less likely to use workarounds).

> ### Get Policy Languages, Updates, and More on Nolo.com
>
> This book is filled with sample policy language you can use to create your own technology policies. You can access it in digital form—along with an acknowledgement form—at this book's companion page at www.nolo.com. (See the appendix for a link to the dedicated page for this book.) You'll find other useful information on that page, too, such as updates and blog posts.

Review and Revise Policies

Once you've come up with draft policies, get some feedback. Ask the IT department and your company's managers to read them; they are the ones who are going to have to actually enforce the policies and field employee questions. They can let you know whether they think it will be difficult to implement a particular policy.

After you've considered this feedback and revised your policies, it's time to get a final review from a lawyer to be sure your technology policies are legally sound and up to date. Technology—and the legal rules governing it—changes at the speed of light. A lawyer can help you make sure your policies are current and effective. A final legal review like this shouldn't take much time (or cost much money).

Distribute Policies and Acknowledgment Forms

Now, it's time to pass out the policies. You should follow that with a meeting where you explain the policies and answer any questions employees might have. Tell employees that the company expects them to read the policies and abide by them, and ask employees to sign an acknowledgment form to that effect. An acknowledgment form is available on this book's companion page on www.nolo.com. See the appendix for the link).

Lessons From the Real World

Adopting technology policies doesn't make your company liable for employee abuse.

It all started when David Sigler yelled at Thomas Kobinsky for letting his child relieve himself in the Sigler's yard. Kobinsky struck back by using his work computer to place public ads for a business Sigler didn't have, order products and subscriptions for the Siglers, and search the Internet for information about them. He also called their workplace on his company cell phone.

The Siglers sued Kobinsky and his employer, CUNA Mutual Insurance Society (CUNA), apparently the deeper pocket. The Siglers argued that, because CUNA had a policy forbidding personal use of computer resources, and because it had previously disciplined a number of employees for Internet offenses, it had a legal duty to monitor employees and review their Internet activities.

A Wisconsin court of appeals rejected the Siglers' claims. The court found that it wasn't reasonably foreseeable that giving employees Internet access would result in Kobinsky's bizarre revenge campaign. The court also found that allowing the lawsuit to proceed would expand liability to such an extent that all employers would be turned into insurers of their employees' online conduct. Having policies and requiring employees to certify that they had read and would comply with those policies was enough to meet the employer's general duty of care to the public.

Sigler v. Kobinsky and CUNA Mutual Insurance Society, 762 N.W. 2d 706 (2008).

CAUTION

Acknowledgment forms may be legally required. Acknowledgment forms may look like overkill or a simple exercise in paperwork, but they are a vitally important part of your technology strategy. Currently, at least one state requires employers to get written consent from employees before monitoring their email and Internet use, and other states consider similar legislation every year. Even if they aren't legally required where your company does business, acknowledgment forms ensure that employees understand the rules for electronic communications, which will result in fewer violations of those rules and more protection for your company if it ever has to defend a decision to read employee communications.

It's a good idea to meet with employees to discuss any changes or additions to those policies. Use of technology is an area of major interest to employees, and one in which you may meet resistance. At a meeting, you can explain why the company needs these policies and what employees will have to do to comply.

Enforce Policies

Your policies are only as good as the paper they're printed on unless your company puts them into action. Ignoring policy violations is a quick way to undo all of your work. Not only does it signal to employees that they don't have to follow the rules, but it also creates extra legal exposure. Adopting a policy shows that your company understands the risks of misusing a particular technology. If it ignores policy violations, your company is essentially saying, "We understand that this could create problems, but we've decided not to do anything about it."

For example, suppose company policy says employees will be issued hands-free equipment and must use it when driving and talking on a cell phone for business. The company hands out cell phones, but decides to put off purchasing headsets until the next fiscal year. An employee hits a pedestrian while taking a sales call. Here's what the pedestrian's lawyer might ask the human resources manager: "You wrote these policies, correct? And you said employees have to use hands-free technology because your company recognizes that's safer than allowing them to use handheld phones while driving, right? But your company never purchased hands-free devices, did it? And now, my client has been permanently injured because your company didn't want to spend $500, isn't that right?"

Review Policies and Update If Necessary

If you're in charge of keeping your company's employee handbook up to date, you probably don't read it from cover to cover when a review is required; you review only policies that may need to be changed because of a court ruling, new statute, or change in company practice. The truth is that most company policies aren't going to change from year to year.

In the technology arena, however, things change quickly and you may find these policies need review once or twice a year. When you adopt a new policy or change the company's existing policy, meet with employees to explain what's new. As you did when you initially rolled out your tech policies, you should give employees time to read the policy, tell them why it was adopted, and answer any questions they might have. You should also prepare a new acknowledgment form.

Keep in mind, too, that this is just the beginning. Every year, there are new technology-related concerns on the horizon and your company's policies should address these issues as soon as they hit your radar screen.

Considering New Technology?

After reading this book, you'll have a good idea of the kinds of issues you need to consider and address in your tech policies. You can use that expertise to help inform the company's decisions about new technology. Rather than just introducing a new gadget and waiting for the fallout, your company can plan ahead to avoid future problems. Here are some questions to brainstorm when your company is looking into new electronic resources:

- Why do we need this technology? Knowing how you want employees to use a particular device will help you make more informed decisions about purchasing, functionality, and appropriate limits for employees.
- Will we supply it for employees? If so, you'll have to think about how you will decide who gets one and whether you will limit personal use. If not, will you reimburse employees who purchase their own device? How will you limit security risks of employees linking to your network from, or keeping business information on, a personal device?
- Who will use this technology? If only the most senior management will be using a particular device, for example, your company may decide to forgo monitoring or extensive rules about personal use.
- What risks are associated with this technology? Are there new data security issues to consider? Safety concerns? A high risk of theft (as is true with many smaller devices) or abuse?
- What records does the device create? Because most technology creates a record, you'll need to consider whether your company should keep those records and in what form.
- Do we want to monitor employee use of the technology? If so, you'll need to make sure you have the resources and capability to handle it.

Computers and Software

In This Chapter:

Policy Provisions for Computers and Software

☐ Use of Computer Equipment

☐ Encryption and Encoding

☐ Software Use

Although many of us think of computers and the Internet as being joined at the hip, the computer—sans the Internet connection—remains a crucial business tool. Half of all U.S. employees work at computers, where they write documents, use spreadsheets, design graphics and artwork, put together presentations, track financial records, and more.

Because employees do the bulk of their work—and store it—on company computers, your company's policies must address several concerns. First, your company must be able to access its digital records and data if and when it needs to. Second, your company must protect its investments and make sure that computer equipment is not misused. Finally, your company must make sure that employees don't illegally use, copy, or download software programs.

The High Cost of Software Piracy

The value of pirated software worldwide climbed to more than $63 billion in 2011, according to the Business Software Alliance. The software piracy rate—a ratio that compares the cost of legitimately purchased software to the cost of stolen software—was 42%, which means that for every $100 sold in legitimate software, another $75 or so worth of pirated software was sold. These international figures are significantly higher than the figures for the U.S., which has a piracy rate of 19% and saw almost $10 billion in pirated software sold in 2011. You can find out more at the Alliance's website, www.bsa.org.

Computers

Your computer use policy must address only a few basic issues; most of the details can be left to your other policies on specific computer activities such as email (discussed in Chapter 3), Internet access (discussed in Chapter 4), instant messaging (discussed in Chapter 5), and blogs and social media (discussed in Chapters 6 and 7).

Appropriate Use of the System

You should make sure employees know that their computers are company property, which the company may access at any time. In other words, the company has unfettered access to unfinished novels, vacation photos, spreadsheets of eBay sales, or any other private data that an employee saves to a company machine or hard drive. You should also require employees to limit their personal use of the computer system. The policy below spells out those limitations.

The Company may provide you with computer equipment and access to the Company's network in order to perform your job.

Use of Computer Equipment

The Company's computer equipment and network are intended for business use. You may use the Company's computer equipment for occasional personal purposes, but you may do so during nonwork hours only. Excessive personal use of the Company's computer equipment, even during nonwork hours, will be cause for discipline.

The Company has the ability to access and review all information stored on the Company's computer equipment and network. The Company reserves the right to perform such an inspection at any time, for any reason. You should not expect that any files, records, or other data stored on the Company's equipment and network will be private, even if you attempt to protect its privacy (for example, by using a password or designating it as "personal").

Lessons From the Real World

Employee's home computer can be searched.

Robert Zieminski was an executive at TBG Insurance Services Corporation. TBG gave him two computers to use for work: One sat on his desk at the office, and the other was at his home.

Zieminski signed a company policy regarding use of its electronic and telephone equipment, which said in part that he would use the computers for business purposes only, that he would not use the equipment for "improper, derogatory, defamatory, obscene, or other inappropriate purposes," and that improper use of the computers could result in discipline, including termination. He also agreed that the company could monitor his computer use "as needed," and that his computer communications were not private.

The company fired Zieminski, claiming that he had repeatedly accessed pornographic sites on the Internet from his work computer. Zieminski filed a wrongful termination lawsuit, alleging that the company really fired him because a large portion of his stock in the company was about to vest; he also said that he never intentionally accessed porn sites, but instead that those sites simply "popped up" on his computer screen.

As part of the lawsuit, TBG asked Zieminski to hand over his home computer. Zieminski agreed to give back the computer, but insisted that he had to delete or destroy some personal information on the computer, which he contended was protected by his right to privacy. Zieminski claimed that, despite the monitoring policy he signed, employees understood that they could use their home computers for personal purposes, and that his computer included tax returns, personal correspondence, and records created by his wife and children. TBG countered that it had to see the computer intact in order to find out whether he accessed the same pornographic sites from home, which would tend to undermine his claim that those sites popped up on his work computer involuntarily.

The California Court of Appeals sided with TBG and required Zieminski to hand over the computer without deleting anything. TBG's policy put Zieminski on notice that his computer use could be monitored, and Zieminski signed that policy. Therefore, he could not argue that he had any reasonable expectation of privacy in the contents of his computer, even though it was in his home and was used by his family members.

TBG Insurance Service Corp v. Superior Court of Los Angeles County, 96 Cal.App.4th 4443 (Cal. App. 2nd District, 2002).

CAUTION

If you find child pornography on company computers, you may have a duty to report it. According to the National Conference for State Legislatures (www.ncsl.org), at least seven states require computer technicians or ISPs to report child pornography they find in the course of their work. These laws don't require monitoring or searching for illegal material, but it must be reported if found. If a company audit or monitoring turns up child pornography or other illegal material on company equipment, talk to a lawyer to find out how to proceed.

Remote Access to the Company's Computer System

If your company's employees work from home or at distant locations, you may have set up a virtual private network or other system by which these employees can access the company's servers.

These systems can be huge time- and money-savers, as they allow employees to get the files and programs they need—and work collaboratively—from a distance. They also allow the company's technical support staff to access remote employee computers and help resolve problems from afar.

These systems typically have strong security features to ensure that only authorized users can get into the company's electronic business. So, if your company has invested the resources to get one of these systems, you undoubtedly want employees to use it. And, whether or not your company provides remote access, you probably don't want employees taking it upon themselves to download commercial software (or use online programs) that allow them into the company's network through a back door.

If your company has a virtual private network or other system, the last sentence of the second paragraph in the policy below should tell employees how (and who) to ask to have it installed on their remote computers. If not, simply delete this paragraph.

The policy below also bans commercial file sharing or cloud storage services. These services allow employees to upload files to a virtual container, hosted on the provider's servers, which can then be accessed remotely.

A growing number of employers choose to allow employees to use their personal smart phones or tablets for work purposes. If you go this route, often called "BYOD" (bring your own device), and you want to give employees remote access not just to email and calendaring applications, but also to files and documents, you'll need a secure delivery and storage system. But you won't want employees storing your company's information on servers and services over which you have no control. (For more on BYOD policies, see Chapter 9.)

Remote Access

While software and programs that allow users remote access to a computer (for example, access to your home computer from work or your work computer from home) can be convenient, they also present security risks. Therefore, employees are prohibited from using these tools to access their work computers (and the Company's servers and network) from a distance, or to access any outside computer from their work computers, unless specifically authorized by [*name of department that handles technical matters, such as "the IT department"*].

If you need remote access to your work computer from home or another distant location, please ask [*name of department that handles technical matters, such as "the IT department"*] to assist you in loading the appropriate tools and configuring them properly.

Employees are prohibited from using commercial file hosting services, such as Dropbox or Rapid Share, or cloud storage services, for work-related files, unless specifically authorized by [*name of department that handles technical matters, such as "the IT department."*]

Remote Access Hack Leads to Lawsuits

After a number of restaurants faced hacking incidents in which customers' credit card information was stolen electronically, they sued the maker of their POS computer systems (Radiant Systems) and the reseller (Computer World). According to news reports, Computer World installed remote access software in the systems, to allow technicians to troubleshoot technical difficulties remotely. Unfortunately, the remote access channel for all of the systems was protected by the same password: "computer." Given this level of security, it probably wasn't too difficult for the people who hacked the system (and used stolen credit cards for $1.2 million in purchases).

Encryption and Encoding

Some of your company's employees may need to encrypt or encode sensitive information, especially if it is leaving the building virtually (on the Internet) or physically (on a laptop, computer disk, or flash drive, for example). This is particularly true of employees who handle private customer or client data, medical records, and so on.

However, many employees have no business need to use encryption or encoding software. In that situation, the only real reason to use such software is to prevent their employer from reading their documents or email messages. It's wise to inform employees that encryption—except under the direction of the company—is prohibited. This policy reinforces the principle that employees should have no expectation of privacy in data on their computer (encrypted or otherwise); and that the company has the right to access all computer data all of the time. Further, prohibiting encryption lowers the possibility that company trade secrets, know-how, and data will disappear.

Encryption and Encoding

You may not encrypt or encode any files, data, or other information stored on the Company's computer equipment or network. If your job requires you to use encryption or encoding software, you may use it only for Company-related reasons and only with the permission of [*position authorized to allow encryption/encoding, such as "the IT director"*].

Software

Some employees mistakenly believe that the company's $699 copy of Adobe InDesign is free for all to use, wherever and whenever they choose. In truth, the company does not own its copy of InDesign: It has paid $699 for a license to use it, usually only on one machine. If the license is violated—by employees or by the employer—the owner of the software can seek damages, often far exceeding the cost of the license, and the company will be on the hook.

Another big problem is software downloads from the Internet. Even if the download is legal (and many aren't; there are plenty of sites offering pirated software), it may well create a security risk for your company. Software downloads may include viruses and other malware that can infect your company's whole system. Typically, the employee isn't even aware of these risks because the download is disguised as a legitimate software program.

To avoid these problems, your software policy should ban copying, installing, and downloading software without permission.

Software Use

It is our Company's policy to use licensed software only in accordance with the terms of its license agreement. Violating a license agreement is not only unethical; it is also illegal and can subject the Company to criminal prosecution and substantial monetary penalties.

To help us adhere to this policy, employees may not do any of the following without permission from [*position authorized to approve software use, such as "the IT director"*]:

- Copy any Company software program for any reason.

- Install a Company software program on any computer (including your home computer).

- Install a software program (including software licensed or owned by the employee) on any Company computer.

- Download any software program from the Internet to a Company computer.

The Company may audit Company-issued computers at any time to ensure compliance with this policy.

Lessons From the Real World

Company pays $500,000 to settle software piracy lawsuit.

The Software & Information Industry Association (SIIA), a trade organization for the software and digital content industry, has been very active in pursuing those who pirate its members' products. It goes after not only those who sell illegal copies of software, but also those who use them—including companies that unwittingly violate their licensing agreements.

In January 2008, the SIIA settled a lawsuit against Whittiker Legal Publishing Corporation. The suit claimed that Whittiker had installed and used copies of software made by SIIA member companies (including Adobe, Filemaker, and Symantec) without the proper licenses. Whittiker agreed to pay half a million dollars, destroy the unlicensed software, purchase replacement software, and adopt comprehensive software management policies. Even though the company used a third-party vendor to manage its software needs, Whittiker bore the ultimate legal responsibility for compliance.

Although it isn't clear how SIIA learned of Whittiker's license violations, many of its enforcement actions stem from whistleblowers. The SIAA has an antipiracy program that encourages people to report corporate misuse of software, offering rewards to those whose tips pan out. In 2009, the SIAA paid out $127,000 in reward money to 24 people who reported corporate end-user software and content piracy. You can learn more at the SIIA's website, www.siia.net (select "Anti-Piracy").

CAUTION

Don't forget the acknowledgment form. If your company adopts the computer and software policy covered in this chapter, make sure you require employees to sign an acknowledgment form. You'll find an acknowledgment form and instructions at this book's companion page at Nolo's website; see the appendix for information on accessing the page.

Putting It All Together: Sample Computer and Software Use Policy

Here's a sample policy for computer and software use adopted by a publishing company. Employees use their computers and software all the time, and the company wants to make sure that it doesn't violate its software licensing agreements. The company uses VPN software to allow employees remote access to the company's servers.

Computer and Software Use Policy

The Company may provide you with computer equipment and access to the Company's network in order to perform your job.

Use of Computer Equipment

The Company's computer equipment and network are intended for business use. You may use the Company's computer equipment for occasional personal purposes, but you may do so during nonwork hours only. Excessive personal use of the Company's computer equipment, even during nonwork hours, will be cause for discipline.

The Company has the ability to access and review all information stored on the Company's computer equipment and network. The Company reserves the right to perform such an inspection at any time, for any reason. You should not expect that any files, records, or other data stored on the Company's equipment and network will be private, even if you attempt to protect its privacy (for example, by using a password or designating it as "personal").

Remote Access

While software and programs that allow users remote access to a computer (for example, access to your home computer from work or your work computer from home) can be convenient, they also present security risks. Therefore, employees are prohibited from using these tools to access their work computers (and the Company's servers and network) from a distance, or to access any outside computer from their work computers, unless specifically authorized by the IT director.

If you need remote access to your work computer from home or another distant location, please ask the IT director to assist you in loading the appropriate tools and configuring them properly.

Employees are prohibited from using file hosting services, such as Dropbox or Rapid Share, or cloud storage services, for work-related files, unless specifically authorized by [*name of department that handles technical matters, such as "the IT department."*]

Encryption and Encoding

You may not encrypt or encode any files, data, or other information stored on the Company's computer equipment or network. If your job requires you to use encryption or encoding software, you may use it only for Company-related reasons and only with the permission of the IT director.

Software Use

It is our Company's policy to use licensed software only in accordance with the terms of its license agreement. Violating a license agreement is not only unethical; it is also illegal and can subject the Company to criminal prosecution and substantial monetary penalties.

To help us adhere to this policy, employees may not do any of the following without permission from the IT director:

- Copy any Company software program for any reason.

- Install a Company software program on any computer (including your home computer).

- Install a software program (including software licensed or owned by the employee) on any Company computer.

- Download any software program from the Internet to a Company computer.

The Company may audit Company-issued computers at any time to ensure compliance with this policy.

Email

In This Chapter:

Policy Provisions for Email

☐ Use of the Email System

☐ Email Is Not Private

  ☐ Optional Policy Language for Monitoring That Flags Keywords

  ☐ Optional Policy Language for Random Monitoring

  ☐ Optional Policy Language for "Keylogger" Monitoring

☐ All Conduct Rules Apply to Email

☐ No Solicitation by Email

☐ Professional Tone and Content

☐ Guidelines for Email Writing

☐ Email Security

☐ Retaining and Deleting Email Messages

erhaps more than any innovation covered in this book, email has revolutionized the way we work. Email can be terrifically efficient. It allows us to communicate quickly, send each other documents, work offsite, work in teams that are geographically dispersed, and document negotiations and decisions, all at warp speed.

But email also has its dark side. Every email message creates an electronic record—in effect, a document that a company might have to hand over in a lawsuit. In addition, the apparent informality of email encourages behavior that people might not engage in face to face, like "flaming," circulating inappropriate jokes, or sharing confidential information. And the speed and virtuality of email also make it easier to commit all manner of workplace misconduct, from harassment to trade secret theft.

Email Bankruptcy

According to the Radicati Group, the typical corporate employee who uses email in 2012 sends 36 messages and receives 78 messages (63 of them legitimate) every day. Unfortunately, this number is well above of the 50 emails per day a 2010 Harris Interactive survey showed to be the "magic number," beyond which employees start to feel like they can't keep up. One of the results of this discrepancy: A 2009 survey in the United Kingdom revealed that almost ¾ of employees spend at least an hour each day dealing with email, and that the average employee inbox includes 2,769 saved messages!

Given the size of the pile-up, it's no wonder that some overwhelmed users resort to "email bankruptcy": deleting the entire contents of one's inbox to get a fresh start.

If you're having trouble believing that email can cause this much trouble, consider these statistics:

- Almost half of employees have sent or received emails that include jokes, stories, or pictures of a "questionable" nature (that is, with racy or sexual content, or that are politically incorrect). (2005 Harris Interactive Poll for Fortiva.)

- Six percent of employees have emailed confidential company information to someone they shouldn't have. (Gregg Keizer, "Email Spills Corporate Secrets," *InformationWeek*, December 12, 2005.)
- Although 92% of employees surveyed said that they had never sent an email that put their company at risk, 68% in fact had. (2005 Harris Interactive Poll for Fortiva.)
- More than a quarter of companies in a recent survey have fired an employee for email misuse; most of those terminations were for inappropriate or offensive language and violation of company rules. (2007 Electronic Monitoring & Surveillance Survey, conducted by the American Management Association and The ePolicy Institute.)
- Fifteen percent of companies have faced a lawsuit triggered by employee email, and almost one quarter of companies have had their email subpoenaed by courts and regulators. (2006 Electronic Monitoring & Surveillance Survey, conducted by the American Management Association and The ePolicy Institute.)

To reap the considerable benefits of email while keeping risks to a minimum, your company must adopt a sensible and comprehensive email policy and require employees to sign off on it. This chapter explains everything you'll need to cover, including personal use of email, email monitoring, archiving and retention of messages, rules on appropriate content, and more.

RELATED TOPIC

Information on personal Web-based accounts. This chapter covers only the company's own email system. However, some employees use their company's Internet connection (or use handheld devices such as BlackBerries or iPhones) to send and receive email on their own personal accounts (for example, Hotmail or Yahoo!). You can find more information on this issue in Chapter 4.

Personal Use of Email System

The first decision to make is whether your company will allow employees to send personal email messages—messages to friends and family members, for example, or messages to coworkers about nonwork topics, such as sports, politics, or parties—using the company's equipment. Although some companies ban all personal use of their email systems, a more practical approach is to allow some personal use with restrictions.

What Would You Give Up to Keep Your Email Access?

Many of us use email every day, some of us for hours a day. But how important is email to us? Would we be willing to give up other things we hold dear just to maintain our email access? According to a recent survey, the answer is a resounding "Yes!" Almost 75% of the respondents indicated that email is essential to their lives. So essential that they would be willing to forgo the following to keep it:

- More than half said they would give up chocolate.
- Half said they would give up coffee.
- More than 40% would give up television.
- Almost 40% would give up their cell phones.
- Almost 15% would give up their spouse or significant other.
- 6% would give up their home.

Sharon Gaudin, "Would You Give Up Deodorant or a Spouse for Email?" *InformationWeek*, April 17, 2007.

Prohibiting All Personal Use

Some companies don't want employees to use their email systems for personal messages, period. After all, the equipment belongs to the company, personal messages take employees away from their work and create potential liabilities, and then there's the storage and bandwidth problem. So why not just ban all personal use?

For a simple reason: Everyone will break the rule. Some might not have an Internet connection at home; others might have a message that has to be sent immediately (like "I'll be home late" or "Can you pick up the kids' carpool today"). The truth is that a policy forbidding any personal use of email will probably be violated regularly by everyone from the CEO on down.

Because these policies are so often violated, they are seldom enforced, at least not consistently. Companies rarely have the time and energy to spend monitoring every transmission, then imposing discipline on everyone who sends a personal message. Instead, companies enforce the policy when an employee crosses the line by spending significant time on personal messages, sending large attachments, sending messages that include racial jokes or sexual material, sending out solicitations for a child's fundraising activities or a personal business, and so on. It's much easier—and safer, from a legal standpoint—to ban these types of misconduct rather than any and all personal use.

Any time an employer enforces a policy inconsistently, it takes a legal risk. An employee who is disciplined for violating the policy when others are not could point to that inconsistency as evidence of an illegal motive, such as discrimination or retaliation.

> **EXAMPLE:** Carla complains that her manager, Jim, has been sending her sexually explicit jokes on the company's email system. The company has a policy that prohibits all personal email, but it doesn't monitor employee email and has yet to enforce the policy.
>
> The company begins its investigation by reviewing Carla's and Jim's email accounts. The investigator discovers Jim's harassing messages, but also discovers that Carla occasionally uses the company's email system for family matters, including corresponding with her children's teachers and coaches. The company gives Jim a written warning for misconduct; Carla receives a written warning for violating the company's email

policy. Because Carla already has a written warning for performance problems, she is now ineligible for raises and promotions for a year.

Several weeks later, the company receives a demand letter from Carla's attorney. The claim? That the company retaliated against Carla for complaining of sexual harassment. The letter states that other employees routinely used the email system for personal matters, but Carla was the only one disciplined—and only after she complained of possible sexual harassment. The company's attorney advises it to rescind Carla's written warning immediately and perhaps even consider a small monetary settlement. Even though Carla violated the policy, it looks too much like retaliation to enforce it for the first time against someone who had just raised concerns about harassment.

Inconsistent enforcement based on the content of the message could lead to legal problems as well. For example, if your company bans all personal messages but typically looks the other way when employees send them, it could face a discrimination claim if it disciplines an employee for sending out a message proselytizing for his or her religion or publicizing an upcoming event that has a particular ethnic or racial focus, such as a Cinco de Mayo parade or a conference for African American entrepreneurs.

Your company could even face an unfair labor practices charge if it disciplines only for messages relating to a union or other employee organizations, or to working conditions generally. The National Labor Relations Board, the federal agency that enforces the laws relating to unions and employee organizing, has consistently held that employers who single out these types of messages for discipline while allowing similar messages (for example, allowing messages about other organizations or meetings) could be violating the National Labor Relations Act.

For all of these reasons, policies that ban all personal use are impractical and invite legal exposure.

Allowing Some Personal Use

To balance the company's interest in preventing a lot of personal use of its equipment against employees' desire to send occasional personal messages, consider policy language that allows some personal use. The policy provision below allows employees to send personal messages, but only outside of work hours and only at the company's discretion. It also leaves the company room to discipline an employee who taxes the system by sending files with gigantic attachments, spending hours conversing with friends, or sending "chain letter" correspondence to dozens of recipients.

You can (and should) further limit the types of messages employees may send and put them on notice that using email for harassment, for solicitation, or to transmit confidential information will lead to discipline; see "Content Rules," below.

Use of the Email System

The email system is intended for official Company business. Although you may use the email system occasionally for personal messages, you may do so during nonworking hours only. If you send personal messages through the Company's email system, you must exercise discretion as to the number and type of messages you send. You must also ensure that your personal use of the email system does not interfere in any way with your job duties or performance. Any employee who abuses this privilege may be subject to discipline.

Privacy

Your email policy absolutely must inform employees that their messages are not private and must reserve the company's right to monitor and read messages at any time. Even if your company has no plans to actively monitor employee email, it may one day have to do so if an employee is accused of sending sexually harassing messages, transmitting trade secrets to a competitor, or using email to spread false rumors about another employee, for example.

You might be wondering why your company has to tell employees that it might read email messages that are sent on company equipment, especially if those messages might get the company in legal trouble. The answer lies in the way privacy law works. As applied to workplace issues, privacy law generally balances an employee's reasonable expectations of privacy against the employer's reasons for monitoring, searching, and so on. The more a company can do to diminish employee expectations of privacy, the more legal protection it has when monitoring employee communications. And one of the best ways to do this is by explicitly stating, in a written policy, that email messages are not private.

Perceptions of Employers vs. Employees on Email Privacy

Many employees don't believe that employers have the right to read their email messages, even though virtually every court to consider the issue has found otherwise. According to a 2005 study by the Society for Human Resource Management (SHRM) and careerjournal.com, almost half of the employees surveyed did not agree that employers had the right to read employee email. In the same year, a survey conducted by the American Management Association showed that 55% of companies actually do monitor and review employee email.

Lessons From the Real World

Is an employee's email to an attorney confidential?

One of the bedrock principles of the law is the attorney-client privilege, which protects the confidentiality of conversations between a lawyer and his or her client. In the past, employers had very few ways to get their hands on communications between an employee and a lawyer, which were likely to occur in person or by letter or personal phone call.

Today, however, there are some (admittedly risk-taking) employees who use company email to correspond with a lawyer—about suing the employer whose email system they're using. If the employer recovers those email messages, whether in the normal course of monitoring or as part of preparing to defend a lawsuit the employee later files, can it read them?

Courts have ruled different ways on this issue, depending on whether the employee used a personal or work account to send the messages and on the employer's policies and practices. For example, one New York court found that a doctor who sent email to his lawyer on his employer's system had waived the attorney-client privilege because the employer's policy prohibited personal use of the system and told employees that it monitored employee email. (*Scott v. Beth Israel Medical Center,* 847 N.Y.S. 3d 436 (N.Y. Sup. 2007).) On the other hand, several courts have found that an employee who uses a personal email account for legal correspondence, even if using a company computer, has not waived the privilege, regardless of the employer's monitoring practices and policies. (*Stengart v. Loving Care Agency Inc.,* 990 A.2d 650 (2010); *Curto v. Medical World Communications, Inc.,* 2006 WL 1318387 (E.D. N.Y. 2006). The moral of the story? Just because you have the ability to read an employee's email messages to an attorney doesn't mean you have the legal right to do so: Speak to a lawyer yourself before proceeding.

> **Email Is Not Private**
>
> Email messages, including attachments, sent and received on Company equipment are the property of the Company. We reserve the right to access, monitor, read, and/or copy email messages at any time, for any reason. You should not expect privacy for any email you send using Company equipment, including messages that you consider to be personal, or label with a designation such as "Personal" or "Private."

Monitoring

If your company has monitoring software it plans to use, or if someone will be assigned to read employee email on a regular basis, you should let employees know in your written policy. After all, the purpose of an email policy is not only to allow the company to read those problematic messages after they've been sent, but also to deter employees from sending them in the first place. Telling employees that their messages will be monitored and/or read will almost certainly help accomplish this second goal.

CAUTION

Choose your monitors wisely. Before your company gives anyone unfettered access to their coworkers' email, it should consider this: According to a 2007 survey, one-third of IT administrators admit snooping through employee email, files, and other confidential information. (Manek Dubash, "Study: IT Admins Read Private Email," *PC World*, May 29, 2007.) These employees apparently had very little "need to know," but the opportunity to spy on their coworkers was just too tempting. If you choose to monitor, select your readers with great care—and check up to make sure that they aren't overstepping their authority.

Whether your company should regularly monitor employee email is a tough issue to sort through. Doing so will force employees to take the email policy seriously and thereby make them less likely to send messages that are harassing, threatening, or otherwise in violation of your policy. It's just human nature: We aren't as quick to break the rules if we think we will get caught.

But there are some serious downsides as well, with employee dissatisfaction topping the list. Employees don't want to feel like the company doesn't trust them or plans to check up on their every keystroke. Monitoring also costs time and money. And some employers just find monitoring distasteful. They don't want to be cast in the role of Big Brother.

Ultimately, the company's philosophy, workforce, and needs will determine whether the benefits of monitoring outweigh the disadvantages. If your company has no immediate plans to monitor or read employee email, you need not add additional monitoring language: The provision on privacy, above, is sufficient.

If, however, your company plans to regularly monitor messages, you should add that information to your policy immediately following the privacy provision, above. What your policy should say depends on how your monitoring software works. Here are some sample provisions:

Optional Policy Language for Monitoring That Flags Keywords

In addition, the Company's software automatically searches the messages you send for questionable content, including sexual or racial comments, threats, trade secrets, competitive information, and inappropriate language. Any message deemed questionable will be forwarded to, and read by, Company management.

Optional Policy Language for Random Monitoring

In addition, the Company will select and read employee messages at random to ensure that employees are in compliance with this policy.

Optional Policy Language for "Keylogger" Monitoring

In addition, the Company's monitoring software automatically creates a copy of every message you draft, even if you never send it. Company personnel will regularly read these copies to make sure that no employee violates this policy.

Content Rules

Your policy should tell employees what types of messages are allowed and prohibited. It's also a good idea to remind employees what email is: an electronic record of a communication, which can be saved, printed, forwarded to unknown recipients, and otherwise leave the building.

Harassment, Threats, and Other Misconduct

One of the most common email problems employers face is electronic harassment: sexually explicit content, lewd or racist jokes, and inappropriate stories or name calling via the company's email system. Your policy should make clear that all company policies relating to harassment and other misconduct apply equally to email.

All Conduct Rules Apply to Email

All of our policies and rules of conduct apply to employee use of the email system. This means, for example, that you may not use the email system to send harassing or discriminatory messages, including messages with explicit sexual content or pornographic images; to send threatening messages; or to reveal Company trade secrets.

Software Helps Companies Keep It Clean—and Kind

The investment bank Goldman Sachs has become famous for more than a few things in the recent economic recession, including the foul language in employee email messages. After a Senator read some of them aloud at a Congressional hearing, Goldman decided to clean up its act. According to news reports in July 2010, Goldman now prohibits foul language in email, and enforces the rule with screening software.

But what about companies that are less concerned with outright cursing than with employee email messages that seem curt, unprofessional, or unkind? After all, email is a "cold" medium (one that requires the reader to fill in a lot of blanks, per the classic definition by Marshall McLuhan). This means there's lots of room for incorrect assumptions and misinterpretations.

The search for an electronic solution to this more subtle problem has led to the creation of ToneCheck, a software program that scans email messages for words and phrases that reflect the intensity of eight emotions, including humiliation, anger, and sadness. These instances are flagged with emoticons, giving the writer an opportunity to revise the message to avoid conveying unintended or unprofessional feelings along with the budget forecast or meeting agenda.

Solicitation

Many companies prohibit employees from soliciting other employees —for example, to buy products, support a particular political candidate, donate to a charity, or join a religious group. If your company has a no-solicitation rule, you should consider whether to extend it to use of the email system.

The National Labor Relations Board (NLRB) has held that a company could use its general ban on email solicitation to discipline an employee who sent union-related messages. Although it would be discriminatory to single out union messages for discipline while allowing employees to send messages relating to other organizations, the NLRB found that a larger prohibition on all solicitation for outside groups was legal.

The policy language below prohibits the most common types of solicitation.

No Solicitation by Email

You may not use the email system to solicit others to patronize an outside business or to support an outside organization, a political candidate or cause, or a religious cause. You also may not use the email system to ask employees to donate to a particular charitable cause.

Professional Tone and Content

Your policy should also remind employees that their email messages should be professional and appropriate.

Professional Tone and Content

We expect you to exercise discretion in using electronic communications equipment. When you send email using the Company's equipment, you are representing the Company. Make sure that your messages are professional and appropriate, in tone and content. Remember, although email may seem like a private conversation, email can be printed, saved, and forwarded to unintended recipients. You should not send any email that you wouldn't want your boss, your mother, or our Company's competitors to read.

Netiquette

Your company may want to include some writing guidelines in its policy, especially if it has a lot of entry-level or otherwise inexperienced employees. Because email is seen as informal, some employees send out even work-related messages sprinkled with emoticons and exclamation points, written in all lowercase or capital letters, or filled with acronyms or usages peculiar to the online world. Some employees also make the mistake of sending out email without considering its content or style, only later to regret having expressed anger too hastily or sending a message that doesn't look professional.

You can include as much or as little detail as you like about writing style. Here is a policy provision that includes a handful of common "netiquette" rules:

Guidelines for Email Writing

1. Always spell-check or proofread your email messages. Email is official Company correspondence. Spelling errors in email are all too common, and they look sloppy and unprofessional.

2. Use lowercase and capital letters in the same way that you would in a letter. Using all capital letters is the email equivalent of shouting at someone—and it can be hard on the eyes. Failing to use capital letters at all (to begin a sentence or formal noun) can confuse readers and seem overly cute. Unless you are writing poetry, use standard capitalization.

3. Remember your audience. Although email encourages informal communication, that might not be the most appropriate style to use if you are addressing the CEO of an important customer. And, remember that your email can be forwarded to unintended recipients, some of whom may not appreciate joking comments or informalities.

4. Don't use email for confidential matters. Again, remember the unintended recipient. Your email might be forwarded to someone you didn't anticipate or might be sitting at a printer for all to see. If you need to have a confidential discussion, do it in person or over the phone.

5. Send messages sparingly. There is rarely a need to copy everyone in the Company on an email. Carefully consider who really needs to see the message, and address it accordingly.

6. Always think before you send. Resist the urge to respond in anger, to "flame" your recipient, or to get emotional. Although email gives you the opportunity to respond immediately, you don't have to take it.

7. Don't leave the subject line blank. Always include a brief description, so readers will know what your email is about at a glance. This makes it easier for all of us to manage our email—and makes it more likely that you will receive a response to your message.

8. Don't overuse the "urgent" tag. Mark a message as urgent only if it is truly important and must be answered right away.

Whoops!

Have you ever misaddressed an email, sent an email without a promised attachment, or gotten an email that you considered inappropriate? Well, you're not alone. According to a 2007 *InformationWeek* survey of more than 700 employees:

- 15% said they'd received an email sent in anger.
- 13% said they'd gotten flirtatious email.
- 23% said they'd received email they considered politically incorrect.
- 20% had sent an email to the wrong person.
- Almost 40% had forgotten to include an attachment in an email they sent.
- A very sad 5% had received a humiliating message that was copied to others.

Anyone can make these mistakes or errors in judgment. Even those who really should know better, like, say, Microsoft, which accidentally sent a reporter an email message with a surprising attachment: an internal dossier its PR firm had compiled on the reporter. The reporter was writing a story on Microsoft's blogging initiative as evidence of the company's effort to be more transparent with the public. Ouch! You can read about in the Epicenter blog at *Wired*'s website, www.wired.com; the story appeared in March 2007.

Viruses and Other Security Threats

Your policy should give employees a few tips to help them avoid launching a virus, Trojan horse, worm, or other electronic threat on your company's email system.

Email Security

To avoid email viruses and other threats, employees should not open email attachments from people and businesses they don't recognize, particularly if the email appears to have been forwarded multiple times or has a nonexistent or peculiar subject heading. Even if you know the sender, do not open an email attachment that has a strange name or is not referenced in the body of the email—it may have been transmitted automatically, without the sender's knowledge.

If you believe your computer has been infected by a virus, worm, or other security threat to the Company's system, you must inform the IT department immediately.

Employees may not share their email passwords with anyone, including coworkers or family members. Revealing passwords to the Company's email system could allow an outsider to access the Company's network.

Retention and Deletion

Email messages create electronic records. Your email policy must tell employees how to manage those records—that is, which records to keep and which to delete.

Email messages often include important company records that it either should or is legally required to retain. For example, if applicants apply for a job by email, those email messages are hiring records that, like other hiring records, must be kept for three years. Of course, your company will also want to retain electronic contracts, agreements, records of negotiations, consent forms, and so on.

On the other hand, the great majority of email messages sent and received by your company's employees can—and should—be deleted as soon as they are dealt with. Email messages take up a lot of virtual space, and employees who are email packrats can quickly overload your company's storage capacity.

What's more, your company can be required to produce email messages if it is sued, just as it has to hand over paper documents. The more messages your employees keep, the more messages your company will have to comb through—and possibly hand over—if it is faced with a lawsuit. The Federal Rules of Civil Procedure (FRCP), which set the ground rules for federal lawsuits, were recently amended to require parties to a lawsuit to hand over electronic evidence just like any other evidence, not only when the other party asks for it in discovery but also as part of their pretrial disclosures.

However, the FRCP also acknowledge that electronic evidence is different from regular paper documents, in that it may be difficult to access because it's been destroyed in the regular course of business. Many companies have a practice of deleting email messages and writing over backup tapes after a certain period of time. A company won't face sanctions or penalties for failing to hand over electronic evidence if that evidence was destroyed because of the routine, good-faith operation of an electronic information system. If, for example, your company's email program automatically purges email messages after a certain number of days and reuses its storage capacity by writing over older information, it won't face legal trouble if it can't hand over messages that were destroyed in the regular course of business.

This protection doesn't extend to evidence that's destroyed after the company knows that it is (or might soon be) facing a lawsuit, however. Once this happens, the company has a legal duty to preserve all evidence that might be relevant to the case, including email messages and other electronic information. (This is commonly referred to as a "litigation hold.") If your company faces litigation, it will have to immediately override its usual purge procedures and make sure it hangs on to every applicable document.

Lessons From the Real World

Destroying email messages can be very costly.

Laura Zubulake was an equities trader at UBS Warburg. After she was fired, she sued UBS for sex discrimination, failure to promote, and retaliation. During the lawsuit, she asked UBS to hand over email messages that she claimed included biased comments about her by UBS decision makers.

UBS protested that it would cost hundreds of thousands of dollars to retrieve and review its email messages to decide which it had to hand over. The court decided that UBS would have to hand over all relevant messages that were still readily available, but that Zubulake would have to pay part of the estimated cost of restoring backup tapes. Several orders later, it became apparent that some relevant email messages had been deleted after the lawsuit began, against the court's instructions.

The court found that these email messages had been destroyed willfully. As a result, the court ordered UBS to pay some of Zubulake's pretrial costs. More importantly, the court instructed the jury that UBS had destroyed the email messages, and that the jury could conclude that the messages would have been harmful to UBS's case. After hearing all of the evidence as well as this instruction about the missing emails, the jury awarded more than $29 million to Zubulake.

Zubulake v. UBS Warburg L.L.C., 229 F.R.D. 422 (S.D. N.Y. 2004); Eduardo Porter, "UBS Ordered to Pay $29 Million in Sex Bias Lawsuit," *The New York Times,* April 7, 2005.

Retaining and Deleting Email Messages

Because email messages are electronic records, certain messages must be retained for compliance purposes. Please refer to our record-keeping policy for guidance on which records must be kept, and for how long. If you have any questions about whether and how to retain a particular email message, please ask your manager.

Because of the large volume of emails our Company sends and receives each day, we discourage employees from storing large numbers of email messages that are not subject to the retention rules explained above. Please make a regular practice of deleting email messages once you have read and/or responded to them. If you need to save a particular message, you may print out a paper copy, archive the email, or save it on your hard drive or disk. The Company will purge email messages that have not been archived after _____ days.

The Company may have occasion to suspend our usual rules about deleting email messages (for example, if the Company's is involved in a lawsuit requiring it to preserve evidence). If this happens, employees will be notified of the procedures to follow to save email messages. Failing to comply with such a notice could subject the Company to serious legal consequences, and will result in discipline, up to and including termination.

CAUTION
Don't forget the acknowledgment form. If your company adopts the email policy covered in this chapter, make sure you require employees to sign an acknowledgment form. You'll find a sample acknowledgment form and instructions in at this book's companion page on Nolo's website; see the appendix for instructions on accessing the page.

Lessons From the Real World

Employer has a duty to stop online harassment.

Tammy Blakey was a pilot for Continental Airlines. In 1991, she began complaining that her male coworkers were leaving pornographic pictures in her cockpit and other work areas, and were making vulgar, gender-based remarks to her. Eventually, she filed a lawsuit against Continental for failing to stop this harassment.

While the lawsuit was proceeding, a group of male pilots began posting derogatory remarks about Blakey on an online computer bulletin board for Continental employees. Blakey sought to amend her complaint to add these comments as additional examples of harassment and defamation.

The New Jersey Supreme Court found that Blakey could sue based on the electronic bulletin board comments. Although an employer doesn't have a duty to monitor its employees, the court found, it does have a duty to stop harassment it already knows about—including harassment that takes place online.

Blakey v. Continental Airlines, 751 S.2d 538 (N.J. 2000).

Putting It All Together: Sample Email Policy

Here's a sample email policy for a large financial services company. The company has had some problems with employees sending inappropriate email messages in the past, so it uses software that monitors keywords. It also prohibits all forms of employee solicitation, even for charitable causes. Because many of its employees are relatively new to the work world, the company has decided to adopt the netiquette guidelines as well.

Email Policy

Use of the Email System

The email system is intended for official Company business. Although you may use the email system occasionally for personal messages, you may do so during nonworking hours only. If you send personal messages through the Company's email system, you must exercise discretion as to the number and type of messages you send. You must also ensure that your personal use of the email system does not interfere in any way with your job duties or performance. Any employee who abuses this privilege may be subject to discipline.

Email Is Not Private

Email messages, including attachments, sent and received on Company equipment are the property of the Company. We reserve the right to access, monitor, read, and/or copy email messages at any time, for any reason. You should not expect privacy for any email you send using Company equipment, including messages that you consider to be personal, or label with a designation such as "Personal" or "Private."

In addition, the Company's software automatically searches the messages you send for questionable content, including sexual or racial comments, threats, trade secrets, competitive information, and inappropriate language. Any message deemed questionable will be forwarded to, and read by, Company management.

All Conduct Rules Apply to Email

All of our policies and rules of conduct apply to employee use of the email system. This means, for example, that you may not use the email system to send harassing or discriminatory messages, including messages with explicit sexual content or pornographic images; to send threatening messages; or to reveal Company trade secrets.

No Solicitation by Email

You may not use the email system to solicit others to patronize an outside business or to support an outside organization, a political candidate or cause, or a religious cause. You also may not use the email system to ask employees to donate to a particular charitable cause.

Professional Tone and Content

We expect you to exercise discretion in using electronic communications equipment. When you send email using the Company's equipment, you are representing the Company. Make sure that your messages are professional and appropriate, in tone and content. Remember, although email may seem like a private conversation, email can be printed, saved, and forwarded to unintended recipients. You should not send any email that you wouldn't want your boss, your mother, or our Company's competitors to read.

Guidelines for Email Writing

1. Always spell-check or proofread your email messages. Email is official Company correspondence. Spelling errors in email are all too common, and they look sloppy and unprofessional.

2. Use lowercase and capital letters in the same way that you would in a letter. Using all capital letters is the email equivalent of shouting at someone—and it can be hard on the eyes. Failing to use capital letters at all (to begin a sentence or formal noun) can confuse readers and seem overly cute. Unless you are writing poetry, use standard capitalization.

3. Remember your audience. Although email encourages informal communication, that might not be the most appropriate style to use if you are addressing the CEO or an important customer. And, remember that your email can be forwarded to unintended recipients, some of whom may not appreciate joking comments or informalities.

4. Don't use email for confidential matters. Again, remember the unintended recipient. Your email might be forwarded to someone you didn't anticipate or might be sitting at a printer for all to see. If you need to have a confidential discussion, do it in person or over the phone.

5. Send messages sparingly. There is rarely a need to copy everyone in the Company on an email. Carefully consider who really needs to see the message, and address it accordingly.

6. Always think before you send. Resist the urge to respond in anger, to "flame" your recipient, or to get emotional. Although email gives you the opportunity to respond immediately, you don't have to take it.

7. Don't leave the subject line blank. Always include a brief description, so readers will know what your email is about at a glance. This makes it easier for all of us to manage our email—and makes it more likely that you will receive a response to your message.

8. Don't overuse the "urgent" tag. Mark a message as urgent only if it is truly important and must be answered right away.

Email Security

To avoid email viruses and other threats, employees should not open email attachments from people and businesses they don't recognize, particularly if the email appears to have been forwarded multiple times or has a nonexistent or peculiar subject heading. Even if you know the sender, do not open an email attachment that has a strange name or is not referenced in the body of the email—it may have been transmitted automatically, without the sender's knowledge.

If you believe your computer has been infected by a virus, worm, or other security threat to the Company's system, you must inform the IT department immediately.

Employees may not share their email passwords with anyone, including coworkers or family members. Revealing passwords to the Company's email system could allow an outsider to access the Company's network.

Retaining and Deleting Email Messages

Because email messages are electronic records, certain messages must be retained for compliance purposes. Please refer to our record-keeping policy for guidance on which records must be kept, and for how long. If you have any questions about whether and how to retain a particular email message, please ask your manager.

Because of the large volume of emails our Company sends and receives each day, we discourage employees from storing large numbers of email messages that are not subject to the retention rules explained above. Please make a regular practice of deleting email messages once you have read and/or responded to them. If you need to save a particular message, you may print out a paper copy, archive the email, or save it on your hard drive or disk. The Company will purge email messages that have not been archived after 90 days.

The Company may have occasion to suspend our usual rules about deleting email messages (for example, if the Company is involved in a lawsuit requiring it to preserve evidence). If this happens, employees will be notified of the procedures to follow to save email messages. Failing to comply with such a notice could subject the Company to serious legal consequences, and will result in discipline, up to and including termination.

4

Internet Use

In This Chapter:

Policy Provisions for Employee Internet Use

☐ Personal Use of the Internet

☐ Prohibited Uses of the Internet

☐ No Personal Posts Using Company Equipment

Internet Use Is Not Private:

    ☐ Alternative 1: Privacy Policy Reserving the Right to Monitor

    ☐ Alternative 2: Privacy Policy for Companies That Monitor Regularly

☐ Don't Use Personal Email Accounts for Work

Access to Personal Email Accounts:

    ☐ Alternative 1: No Access to Personal Email Accounts

    ☐ Alternative 2: Rules for Accessing Personal Email Accounts

    ☐ Optional Policy Language for Blocking Access to Personal Email

    ☐ Optional Policy Language for Keylogger Software

t's no wonder that many of us have become blasé about the Internet. It is so ubiquitous, so useful, and so essential to our work that it's hard to believe that we once had to manually track shipments, book travel, locate information, map a trip, go shopping, or conduct research without it.

As most businesses are aware, however, allowing employees unlimited Internet access poses problems and threats. As a virtual gateway in and out of the company, the Internet tempts employees to spend work time on personal pursuits like bargain hunting, checking sports scores, joining chat rooms, checking their personal email accounts, or social networking pages, and even looking for a new job. In addition, employees can use the Internet to access inappropriate material—for example pornography, gambling, and hate speech—which is often deemed offensive by coworkers.

Where Employees Go Online

According to a 2006 survey by Websense, more than 60% of employees admitted to visiting personal websites at work, for an average of slightly more than three hours total per week. What types of sites did they visit? The most frequented nonwork sites were map sites, followed by news sites and weather sites. Banking, travel, and shopping sites were close behind.

Of course, a lot has changed on the Internet since 2006, the year Twitter was launched and only a couple of years after Facebook had been created in a dorm room. A 2012 survey by salary.com revealed that Facebook was by far the most popular personal site accessed at work, followed by LinkedIn. Remember MySpace? Neither did anyone who took the survey, but Pinterest and Twitter also made the top ten list.

Employee access to the Web can also inadvertently result in damage to the company's computer system and software, from viruses, spyware, and so on. In fact, experts say that more system attacks are launched on companies today via employee Internet surfing than through email.

Finally, the Internet provides a backdoor by which employees can send information out of the company, whether by transmitting company information through personal email or posting personal comments to outside sites, which can then be traced back to your company.

Do We Have Al Gore to Thank?

Most of the innovations discussed in this book rely on the Internet, known in previous incantations as the World Wide Web or the Information Superhighway. And we all know who invented the Internet ... or do we?

In the run-up to the 2000 election, Al Gore was said to have claimed that he invented the Internet. But it turns out (1) he never said that, and (2) he wouldn't have been too far wrong if he did.

What Gore actually said, in answering a question from CNN's Wolf Blitzer as to why American voters should choose him over his primary competitor Bill Bradley, was that he "took the initiative in creating the Internet." And so he did: Among many other things, he drafted and sponsored the High Performance Communication and Computing Act of 1991, which led to the National Information Infrastructure and the development of Mosaic, a Web browser many believe to have begun the Internet boom of the 1990s.

Gore later made fun of his statement on *Late Night with David Letterman*, giving as number nine of his top ten list of rejected Gore-Lieberman campaign slogans, "Remember, America, I gave you the Internet and I can take it away!"

Personal Use of the Internet

Banning all personal use of the Internet leads to the same problems—employee resentment, selective enforcement, and so on—as banning all personal email. (See Chapter 3 for more information.) A more sensible approach is to allow limited personal use of the Internet during lunch, breaks, or other nonwork hours, as long as that use is not excessive and does not violate the policy's other prohibitions (see "Prohibited Uses of the Internet," below). This will help you not only avoid the problems that an outright ban can create, but also ensure that employees spent more of their work hours doing what your company is actually paying them to do, rather than bidding on eBay auctions or looking for their house on Google Earth.

After Black Friday Comes Cyber Monday

The day after Thanksgiving has been called "Black Friday," a reference to either the heavy traffic (and ensuing headaches) or the bottom-line profit associated with the biggest shopping day of the year. Those who prefer to shop online apparently do so on "Cyber Monday," the first business day after Thanksgiving, when employees return to their workplace computer terminals.

How much shopping do employees do? Challenger, Gray, and Christmas (an outplacement firm—and yes, that is their real name) estimated that 68 million employees would do some holiday shopping online on Cyber Monday, 2007. If each of those employees spent only 12 minutes shopping, it could cost companies $488 million in lost productivity.

And if those 12 minutes stretched into two full days? According to a survey conducted by the nonprofit ISACA, half of the employees surveyed planned to shop online from work in November and December 2009. On average, employees planned to spend more than 14 hours shopping online, from work, during this time period. The same survey found that one in ten employees who has a mobile work device (such as a BlackBerry) planned to use it for holiday shopping.

Personal Use of the Internet

Our network and Internet access are for official Company business. Employees may access the Internet for personal use only outside of work hours and only in accordance with the other terms of this policy. An employee who engages in excessive Internet use, even during nonwork hours, may be subject to discipline.

Prohibited Uses of the Internet

Your policy should tell employees what types of Internet activities and sites are forbidden, what types of downloads and streaming activities are prohibited, and what restrictions the company places on employee postings to other sites.

Prohibited Sites and Downloads

Start by listing the types of electronic information that employees may not access from work. In addition to banning sites with offensive material (such as pornography and violent images), you should ban two types of downloads: those that violate the law—such as inappropriate use of copyrighted material, stolen music files, unlicensed software programs—or those that could infect your company's system—for example, files that may contain viruses or other system threats.

In addition, your company must also consider its tech capacity limits. Streaming audio or video—for example, listening to Internet radio stations or watching live sport events—can quickly overload your company's systems. If that's the case at your company, you'll want to add language banning these uses in your policy.

If your company blocks employee access to particular sites or types of sites using a technological solution—for example, filtering software—you should let employees know that their ability to access a site doesn't necessarily mean it's appropriate for viewing. (If your company doesn't use blocking software, simply delete the last paragraph of this section.)

Prohibited Uses of the Internet

Employees may not, at any time, access the Internet using Company equipment for any of the following purposes:

- To view websites that offer pornography, gambling, or violent imagery, or are otherwise inappropriate in the workplace.

- To operate an outside business, online auction, or other sales site; solicit money for personal purposes; or otherwise act for personal financial gain or profit.

- To download or copy software, games, text, photos, or any other works in violation of copyright, trademark, or other laws.

- To stream, run, or download any non-Company-licensed software program without the express consent of the IT department.

- To stream, run, or download music, video, games, minidesktop applications (widgets), or any form of multimedia, from the Internet.

- To read, open, or download any file from the Internet without first screening that file for viruses using the Company's virus detection software.

If you believe that your job may require you to do something that would otherwise be forbidden by this policy, ask your manager how to proceed.

To ensure that employees comply with this policy, we use software that will block your access to many prohibited sites. However, some inappropriate websites may escape detection by the software: The fact that you can access a particular site does not necessarily mean that site is appropriate for workplace viewing.

Lessons From the Real World

Is Internet sex addiction a disability?

James Pacenza worked for IBM for 19 years until he was fired after a coworker witnessed a chat room discussion about sex on Pacenza's computer screen. Pacenza claimed that his termination was illegal because, among other things, he visited Internet chat rooms as a way to "self-medicate" his disability.

Pacenza, a veteran of the Vietnam War, suffered from post-traumatic stress disorder and depression. Pacenza claimed that IBM shouldn't have fired him because Internet sex addiction was a manifestation of his disability. Therefore, the company's decision to fire him—rather than working with him to come up with a reasonable accommodation—was discriminatory.

Not surprisingly, IBM contended that Pacenza was fired for violating its policy on Internet misuse, and that it had no obligation to accommodate his desire to engage in sexual chat room discussions.

Pacenza lost his case, but the question of Internet addiction as a disability lingers on, whether the claimed addiction is to the Internet itself (for someone who can't be offline for more than a few hours or can't stop checking email) or to the Internet's ability to bring other addictive material directly to the user (for example, porn sites for a sex addict or gaming sites for a gambling addict). But that probably won't last forever. Today, you can find therapists who specialize in treating Internet addiction, scholarly articles on the problem, and even 12-step programs to combat the addiction (ironically, some are available online). And, "Internet Use Disorder," will be recommended for further study in the DSM-5, the definitive guide to mental disorders used by mental health professionals.

Even if Internet sex addiction becomes a legally recognized disability, however, employers who utilize blocking software have little to worry about: One proposed "reasonable accommodation" is to make sure that employees can't access inappropriate sites—particularly porn sites—while at work, which is exactly what blocking software is designed to accomplish.

Prohibited Posts to Other Sites

When employees state their personal opinions by, for example, posting a comment to a blog or forum, those opinions could mistakenly be attributed to their employer—for example, if the employee or the employee's email address gives it away. In addition, any transmission may be traceable back to your company computers (or to an Internet Protocol address, a unique number that points to your company as a source).

At the same time, employees who post anything about your company's products absolutely must identify themselves and their employment relationship to your company. Rules adopted by the Federal Trade Commission in 2009 require any endorser of a product—including those who post online reviews or discuss products on online discussion boards—to reveal their relationship to the product's maker, if applicable. This includes employees who post content online about the things your company sells. Chapter 6 includes policy language to deal with this issue; you needn't include it here because this policy prohibits all personal posts using company equipment, period.

Your policy should prohibit employees from posting to other sites using company equipment. (For information on employee posts from personal computers to blogs, websites, or third-party sites, see Chapter 6.) Some of your company's employees might post online as part of their jobs. For example, a publicist or social media specialist might routinely post to other sites in their official capacities as employees. If your company has positions like these, you might want to add a sentence to the end of this part of the policy, such as "If you believe your job requires you to post online in your official capacity as a company employee, please speak to your supervisor."

No Personal Posts Using Company Equipment

Employees may not use the Company's equipment to transmit their personal opinions by, for example, posting a comment to a blog or contributing to an online forum. Even if you don't identify yourself as a Company employee, your use of Company equipment could cause your opinion to be mistaken for the Company's view.

Lessons From the Real World

To the virtual barricades! When avatars strike.

Apparently, the Hollywood writers' strike wasn't the only work stoppage in the Fall of 2007: Italian employees of IBM also went on strike. At least, their avatars did—in Second Life.

Second Life (www.secondlife.com) is a virtual world in which real people and real companies can role-play—that is, maintain a virtual presence with visual representations (avatars) and real estate. For example, IBM, like many businesses, maintains its own "campus" or "island" within the Second Life environment.

According to press reports, the trade union representing IBM's workers in Italy requested a pay increase and IBM responded by cutting performance bonuses. The union then solicited a virtual strike by Second Lifers; it asked Residents to man the picket lines and occupy IBM's Second Life real estate.

This virtual occupation—over 1,800 Residents stormed the IBM campus—must have had some success. Talks with the union resumed, the performance bonuses were reinstated, and the person responsible for the pay cuts resigned. And here's a benefit you don't see from most strikes: Strike organizers won a "NetXplorateur" prize in 2008 from the French Senate, intended to recognize the most exemplary Web-related projects of the year.

Privacy

Just as you did in your email policy, you should tell employees that their Internet use is not private. A policy like this—whether you currently monitor employee Internet usage or just want to reserve the right in the future—may greatly minimize your company's legal exposure.

Here are some examples of situations when you might need to investigate an employee's Internet activity:

- Several employees complain that their manager is viewing pornography on his computer terminal. They claim that the manager has offensive pictures up on his screen when he calls them into his office for meetings or conversations. The manager denies everything.

- Posts to several online investor forums indicate that a publicly traded company will soon release a new product, resulting in a quick jump in its stock price. A few members of the company's management team sell off much of their stock shortly before the rumor is shown to be false.

- An employee's performance has declined significantly, and coworkers claim that he spends most of his time trying to accumulate friends on his Facebook page. The employee claims that his job requires him to check social networking sites to see what job applicants have posted about themselves, but he doesn't access those sites from work for personal reasons.

If your company uses monitoring software (according to surveys, nearly ¾ of employers do), you should let employees know. After all, the goal is not just to keep track of where employees go on the Internet, but to stop them from going to inappropriate sites in the first place. Telling employees that they're being watched is sure to cut down on prohibited, unnecessary, and unauthorized surfing.

The first policy, below, simply reserves the right to monitor. The second version tells employees that monitoring is underway.

Alternative 1: Privacy Policy Reserving the Right to Monitor

> **Internet Use Is Not Private**
>
> We reserve the right to monitor employee use of the Internet at any time. You should not expect that your use of the Internet—including but not limited to the sites you visit, the amount of time you spend online, and the communications you have—will be private.

Alternative 2: Privacy Policy for Companies That Monitor Regularly

> **Internet Use Is Not Private**
>
> Our Company uses monitoring software that, among other things, tracks the sites an employee visits and how much time is spent at a particular site. You should not expect that your use of the Internet—including but not limited to the sites you visit, the amount of time you spend online, and the communications you have—will be private.

Personal Web-Based Email

Although most companies have policies that address use of the company's email system (see Chapter 3), many companies have no policy regarding employees accessing their personal email accounts from work using the company's equipment. At first blush, it might seem like overkill to limit an employee's ability to check a personal email account from work. After all, if the company doesn't want employees to send a lot of personal messages on its own system, shouldn't it allow them to access their own accounts, at least during breaks and lunch?

Unfortunately, it's not that simple. Personal email accounts, such as those available from Hotmail, Yahoo!, Comcast, and AOL, are Web-based. When an employee accesses this type of account from work, messages sent and received bypass the employer's security system. This means bad things—such as viruses, Trojan horses, and spyware—can get in, and good things—like trade secrets—can get out, and the company will never know about it.

> **RELATED TOPIC**
>
> **Is your workplace "BYOD"?** This section addresses policy provisions for employee's use of their own personal email accounts, either when accessed using your company's equipment or when used to conduct business. A growing number of companies follow "bring your own device" (BYOD) system, by which employees can use their own mobile devices—smartphones and tablets—to access the company's email, applications, and sometimes documents and files. This is different from the employee using a personal account (rather than a personal device) to conduct business, covered here. For information on BYOD, see Chapter 9.

Doing Business Via Personal Email

Even employees with the best intentions can create huge problems for a company via their personal email accounts. Take, for example, the common practice of employees sending work-related documents or messages to their personal email address. Most employees who do this are simply trying to make it easier to work from home; some are trying to get around an employer system that allows them to save only a limited number of messages by keeping those messages in their personal account. And still other employees automatically forward messages they receive at work to their personal account, to make sure they can access their email while traveling for business. What harm could that cause?

Plenty, as it turns out. Those work documents and messages are stored not on the company's servers but on the Internet, where they could potentially be accessed by people outside the company. What if the employee's ISP scans messages to send targeted advertising to the user? What if someone hacks into the ISP's servers? What if the employee's laptop is stolen, with a saved password that allows the thief easy access to the employee's Web-based account? This is especially problematic if the forwarded information is something the employer has an obligation to keep private, such as medical records, customer information, or company trade secrets.

Beyond the potential theft or exposure of company records, allowing employees to transact company business via their personal email accounts creates another big problem for the company: Some of its business records are out of its control. The company might not even know about key negotiations, discussions, and deals that are carried out on personal email. It won't have those records if it needs to recreate contract talks, review an employee's personnel file, or respond to a subpoena. And, employees may save documents long after they would have been purged from the company's records, which means there could be a "smoking gun" out there that would otherwise have been destroyed.

All companies should adopt a policy prohibiting employees from using their personal email accounts to transact company business. This includes not only using those accounts for business correspondence, but also transmitting any messages or files that might contain confidential information.

Don't Use Personal Email Accounts for Work

Employees may not use their own personal email accounts to transact Company business. This includes storing work-related documents and email messages in your personal email account, sending work to your personal email account, engaging in work-related communications (with customers, clients, or coworkers, for example) using your personal email account, or "bouncing" messages from your Company email to your personal email when you are out of the office.

Although employees may find these practices convenient, they can create significant security problems, expose confidential Company

Don't Use Personal Email Accounts for Work (continued)

> information, and compromise the Company's record-keeping
> obligations. If you work offsite (for example, at home or on business
> travel), please contact the IT department to find out how to safely
> transmit and protect Company information.

Accessing Personal Email Accounts at Work

The risks discussed above give employers very good reasons to simply
prohibit employees from using their Web-based email accounts at
work. However, many companies are uncomfortable with a total
ban. Surveys show that one-half to three-quarters of responding
companies have no policies on access to Web-based email. Some
are probably unaware of the potential problems; others may simply
think a policy banning employee access to their own email accounts
is too Draconian.

Your company will have to decide, based on its culture, level of
trust in its employees, and values, whether to adopt a total ban. Even
if your company decides not to prohibit all access to personal email,
however, it should still have a policy putting some limits on the
practice.

Alternative 1: Banning Access to Personal Email

No Access to Personal Email

Accessing your personal email account from work creates security
risks for the Company's computer system and network. Therefore,
employees may not use Company equipment to access their
personal email accounts.

Alternative 2: Allowing Access to Personal Email

Rules for Accessing Personal Email

Accessing your personal email account from work creates security risks for the Company's computer system and network. To help control these risks, employees must follow these rules when using Company equipment to access their personal email:

You may access your personal email account during nonwork hours only.

Do not open any personal email messages from an unknown sender. Personal email is subject only to the security controls imposed by your provider, which may be less strict than the Company's. If a personal message contains a virus or other malware, it could infect the Company's network.

Before you open any attachment, you must scan it for viruses using the Company's antivirus software.

You may not transact Company business using your personal email account, nor may you transmit any Company documents using your personal email account.

Monitoring or Blocking Personal Email

If your company decides to ban employee access to their personal email accounts, you can use blocking software to prevent employees from accessing common email sites such as Hotmail, Yahoo!, and so on. If your company's monitoring system allows it to see employee messages in their personal email accounts (for example, because you use software that tracks everything the employee types or captures a screenshot of employee computers), you should let employees know.

Be warned, however, that you may not have a legal right to actually read messages sent to and from an employee's personal email account, even if those messages are sent using company equipment. A few courts have held that an employer may not read personal messages (and particularly not messages exchanged with an attorney) in an employee's personal email account. This is especially so if the employer accesses the messages using the employee's password, as captured by monitoring software. Before looking at email messages in an employee's personal account, consult with a lawyer.

The exact language you put in your policy will depend on the type of monitoring or blocking tools your company uses. Here are a couple of examples:

**Optional Policy Language for Blocking Access
to Personal Web-based Email Sites:**

> The Company's security software blocks access to many Web-based email sites. The fact that you can access a Web-based email site does not mean that you are free to check personal email using the Company's equipment, however.

Optional Policy Language for Keylogger Software:

> The Company's monitoring software keeps track of everything you type on your computer. Therefore, although the Company allows employees to access their personal email accounts using Company equipment, employees should not expect any messages they send or view from work to be private.

Lessons From the Real World

Damages may be appropriate against employer who read employee's personal email messages.

While Bonnie Van Alstyne worked at Electronic Scriptorium, Limited (ESL), the president of ESL—Edward Leonard—accessed her personal email account and read her email. Van Alstyne used this personal account for business from time to time, but also had a company email account.

Van Alstyne didn't find out about Leonard's surreptitious reading until she had been fired and filed a lawsuit for sexual harassment and other employment claims against ESL. ESL then sued Van Alstyne for business-related torts and, in the course of discovery in that case, provided several email messages as evidence that had been copied from Van Alstyne's personal account. It later came out that Leonard had accessed Van Alstyne's account "at all hours of the day" and from a variety of locations, and ultimately produced copies of 258 email messages he had taken from that account.

Van Alstyne asked for damages for Leonard's actions. Leonard and ESL were ultimately ordered to pay compensatory damages, punitive damages, and attorney fees and costs. On appeal, the court knocked out the compensatory damages awards because Van Alstyne hadn't proved that she suffered actual damages—out-of-pocket losses caused by the violation. However, the court found that it was appropriate to award punitive damages and attorney fees even if Van Alstyne couldn't prove any actual damages.

Van Alstyne v. Electronic Scriptorium, Limited, 560 F.3d 199 (4th Cir. 2009).

> ⚠ CAUTION
>
> **Don't forget the acknowledgment form.** If your company adopts the Internet policy covered in this chapter, make sure you require employees to sign an acknowledgment form. You'll find a sample acknowledgment form and instructions on this book's companion page at Nolo's website; see the appendix for more information.

Putting It All Together: Sample Internet Policy

Here's a sample Internet use policy adopted by an independent bookstore. The store's buyer uses the Internet frequently, while most employees need Internet access occasionally to answer customer questions, but don't spend much time online. The store doesn't have the time, money, or staff to actively monitor employee Internet use, nor has it invested in monitoring or blocking software. Because it also has limited IT capability, the store has decided to simply prohibit employees from accessing inappropriate sites, downloading or streaming improper materials, participating in outside business ventures, making personal posts, or accessing their personal email accounts from work.

Using the Internet

Personal Use of the Internet

Our network and Internet access are for official Company business. Employees may access the Internet for personal use only outside of work hours and only in accordance with the other terms of this policy. An employee who engages in excessive Internet use, even during nonwork hours, may be subject to discipline.

Prohibited Uses of the Internet

Employees may not, at any time, access the Internet using Company equipment for any of the following purposes:

- To view websites that offer pornography, gambling, or violent imagery, or are otherwise inappropriate in the workplace.

- To operate an outside business, online auction, or other sales site; solicit money for personal purposes; or otherwise act for personal financial gain or profit.

- To download or copy software, games, text, photos, or any other works in violation of copyright, trademark, or other laws.

- To stream, run, or download any non-Company-licensed software program without the express consent of the IT department.

- To stream, run, or download music, video, games, minidesktop applications (widgets), or any form of multimedia, from the Internet.

- To read, open, or download any file from the Internet without first screening that file for viruses using the Company's virus detection software.

If you believe that your job may require you to do something that would otherwise be forbidden by this policy, ask your manager how to proceed.

No Personal Posts Using Company Equipment

Employees may not use the Company's equipment to transmit their personal opinions by, for example, posting a comment to a blog or contributing to an online forum. Even if you don't identify yourself as a Company employee, your use of Company equipment could cause your opinion to be mistaken for the Company's view.

Internet Use Is Not Private

We reserve the right to monitor employee use of the Internet at any time. You should not expect that your use of the Internet—including but not limited to the sites you visit, the amount of time you spend online, and the communications you have—will be private.

Don't Use Personal Email Accounts for Work

Employees may not use their own personal email accounts to transact Company business. This includes storing work-related documents and email messages in your personal email account, sending work to your personal email account, engaging in work-related communications (with customers, clients, or coworkers, for example) using your personal email account, or "bouncing" messages from your Company email to your personal email when you are out of the office.

Although employees may find these practices convenient, they can create significant security problems, expose confidential Company information, and compromise the Company's record-keeping obligations. If you work offsite (for example, at home or on business travel), please contact the IT department to find out how to safely transmit and protect Company information.

No Access to Personal Email

Accessing your personal email account from work creates security risks for the Company's computer system and network. Therefore, employees may not use Company equipment to access their personal email accounts.

Instant Messaging

In This Chapter:

Policy Provisions for Instant Messaging

☐ Alternative 1: No Instant Messaging

☐ Alternative 2: No Use of Consumer Instant Messaging

☐ Alternative 3: Using Consumer Instant Messaging Software

☐ IM Usernames and Passwords

☐ Personal Use of IM

☐ IM Is Not Private

☐ All Conduct Rules Apply to IM

☐ IM Security

☐ Retaining and Deleting Instant Messages

nstant messaging ("IM") is a form of text-based real-time communication. Users operate a software program (referred to as a "client"), which allows them to see who else in their IM network (often called a "buddy list" or "contact list") is online. The user can initiate a conversation with an online contact by sending a message, which triggers a pop-up window on the contact's computer. If the contact responds, a running dialog unfolds on the screen until the conversation ends. All instant messages travel though a server operated by the IM company—for example, when you use America Online Instant Messenger (AIM), all of your text passes through AOL's servers.

Should you allow employees to use IM? If so, will you allow them to use commercial IM software or require them to use an enterprise IM (EIM) system licensed by the company, one designed for business use that incorporates legal and security concerns? What limits—on personal use and content, for example—will you place on employee use of IM? And how will you make sure that important messages transmitted via IM will be saved and available when the company needs them? This chapter explains your company's policy options.

To IM or Not to IM?

IM is a great medium for quick, vital exchanges, such as "contract signed," "shipment didn't arrive this a.m., when can we expect?" or "original order sold out; are 1,000 additional units available?" For that reason, certain business that rely on speed—stock trading and sales are two obvious examples—have quickly adopted IM systems in order to connect the right people, right away.

There are other potential IM benefits for businesses, as well. For example, business users of IM can see who's logged in and immediately direct important questions or concerns to an appropriate person who can handle them quickly. In addition, employees who work offsite can use IM to interact more directly with coworkers than they could by phone or email. And, IM allows employees to multitask: IM software is intended to run in the background, so employees can do other work while still receiving and responding to important instant messages. IM also helps many companies perform more efficiently by eliminating telephone tag, email bounce messages, and even some of the need for business travel.

IM May Increase Productivity

IM can be a distraction for employees. The message notification feature—which shows up on top of everything else on your screen—can be disruptive, and the fact that others know you are online can invite conversations for which you really don't have time. So, you may be surprised to learn that a recent survey showed that employees who use IM report fewer workplace interruptions than those who don't.

Almost 30% of those who responded to the survey used IM at work; interestingly, employees between the ages of 46 and 55 were most likely to do so. IM users were less likely to agree with the statement, "I rarely complete a work task without being interrupted," than nonusers. The survey also found that using IM doesn't increase an employee's overall communication time—in other words, IM replaces other forms of communication rather than adding to them.

R. Kelly Garrett and James N. Danziger, "IM=Interruption Management? Instant Messaging and Disruption in the Workplace," *Journal of Computer-Mediated Communication* 13(1) (2007).

As is true of the other technological innovations covered in this book, however, these advantages don't come without some concerns. Among them are:

- **Security risks.** IM systems can carry files, and hackers have learned how to exploit this feature—particularly on commercial IM systems—to infect users' machines. Once one machine is infected, the malware is usually programmed to propagate by transmitting itself to everyone on the user's contact list. Unlike typical contagions by email which take a day or two, IM virus infections spread in hours.
- **Loss of proprietary information.** As with all forms of communication, IM enables employees to quickly pass your company's proprietary information to third parties. In addition, unless you have a purely internal EIM system, all IMs travel via public third-party servers.
- **Messaging spam (spim).** Just in case your business is not getting enough unsolicited commercial messages, IMs can bring you more of the same—except now it's *instant*.
- **Archiving.** Although some EIMs come with built-in archiving, many consumer IM systems do not automatically archive exchanges (as is done with email). As a result, your company may not be able to produce requested IM documents in a lawsuit.
- **Loss of productivity.** Anyone who has used IM knows it can be a tremendous time sink. And unfortunately, because of the way IM works, it can be hard for the well-mannered to ignore that little pop-up window saying "how RU?" Most of us feel we have to respond at the risk of being rude.
- **Informality.** Something about the format of IM—and the fact that it was developed for use in chat rooms—makes users feel that it's strictly for informal social conversation. This can lead to a lack of professionalism in business-related IM, and to inappropriate jokes, comments, or gossip.

Beyond Informality ... the Saga of Maf54

In one of the most shocking tales of workplace misuse of IM, Mark Foley, the former Republican Congressman from Florida, resigned in 2006 after his sexual communications with former male pages—several of whom had saved the heated IM dialogs—became public.

Foley, identified as "Maf54," called one of the correspondents his "favorite young stud," told the former page he was picturing his "great legs" and "cute butt," and soon was into unprintable territory. (At the same time that these conversations were going on, Foley was also the Chairman of the House Caucus on Missing and Exploited Children, which introduced legislation targeting sexual predators.) Foley initially claimed that the messages he sent were innocuous and accused his opponent of dirty politics. Once several news sources printed excerpts from the saved IMs, Foley apologized and immediately resigned.

Alternative 1: Prohibiting IM

The initial decision your company must make is whether IM—either a commercial or enterprise system—has any place in your business. As you consider your company's options, remember that many of your employees are probably already using IM on their work computers. As a practical matter, this means that banning or placing strict limits on IM amounts to taking away something employees already have—which is much more difficult than preventing them from using it in the first place.

If you wish to halt current use (and future uses), your company must block downloads of consumer IM software and routinely audit employee computers to make sure they aren't breaking the rules. Banning IM may also limit your company's options in communicating with future clients, customers, suppliers, and business partners.

If your company nonetheless decides to ban IM altogether—perhaps your employees don't need to converse in real time, you have no or very few employees who work remotely, and your customers and clients don't expect your employees to be available via IM—you can use the policy language below. (You can also skip the rest of this chapter, which applies only to companies that have decided to allow IM in some form.)

No Instant Messaging

Because of the security risks associated with publicly available IM software, instant messaging is prohibited at our Company. Employees may not download or use personal IM software from the Internet to send or receive instant messages. For example, employees may not use Yahoo! Messenger, Windows Live Messenger, or Google Talk. Violation of this policy will result in discipline, up to and including termination.

Permitting IM

If your company decides against an outright IM ban, it has two primary options: It can allow IM only through its own enterprise software or it can allow employees to use consumer IM software.

Alternative 2: Allowing IM Via Enterprise Software

Using enterprise IM software allows your company to avoid some of the problems associated with publicly available IM systems. Your company controls the system, so it can monitor content, check for viruses and other malware, and control abuse. A company-wide IM system can also automatically save and store IM dialogs. And, because all employees will be on the same IM system, you won't face any compatibility problems. On the other hand, enterprise software generally lacks some of the flexibility associated with consumer IM—in particular, employees can only communicate with each other, not the outside world.

Still, an enterprise IM system is ideal for intracompany communications. If your company goes this route, it may also want to prohibit employees from using consumer IM systems. After all, most of the benefits of using a company system will be lost if you leave the back door open.

No Use of Consumer Instant Messaging Systems

To facilitate communication among employees, our Company has an internal instant messaging (IM) system.

Because of the security risks associated with publicly available IM software, employees may not download or use personal IM software from the Internet to send or receive instant messages. For example, employees may not use Yahoo! Messenger, Windows Live Messenger, or Google Talk. Violation of this policy will result in discipline, up to and including termination.

Alternative 3: Allowing IM Via Consumer IM Software

For most companies, especially those with significant numbers of tech-savvy employees, a common solution is to allow employees to (continue to) use consumer IM software and manage the attendant risks using gateway software—software that allows your company to monitor incoming and outgoing IM, scan messages for content and viruses, and archive IM conversations. If you choose this option, you should require employees to utilize your IT department for installation and maintenance of consumer IM systems.

Using Consumer Instant Messaging Software

Our Company makes instant messaging (IM) capability available to our employees. If you wish to use IM, you must notify the IT department and let them know which publicly available IM software you would like to use. The IT department will download the appropriate software and set up your IM account.

Employees may not download or use any IM software on their own, without going through the IT department. Violation of this policy will result in discipline, up to and including termination.

Usernames

There's a reason most people sending IMs aren't using the names listed on their birth certificates: Their screen names allow them to operate behind a pseudonym, to make a statement or to just illustrate a sense of humor.

This is all well and good behind the closed doors of home, but your company really doesn't want its clients receiving business-related IM from babealicious10 or lostfan1. If you allow employees to use IM, you'll need to make sure they adopt professional, straightforward usernames.

IM Usernames and Passwords

Employees will be assigned an IM user ID and password by the IT department. Employees may not change their user ID without permission.

If you have a personal account with any IM software provider, you may not use Company equipment to access your personal account. You may use only the ID and password provided by the Company.

Personal Use of IM

Will your company limit IM to business use only, or will you permit personal use as well? Banning all personal use of IM has its risks, chief among them that your company will inconsistently enforce that ban. Employees who are disciplined for instant messaging conduct (while others get away with it) may claim that your company engaged in retaliation, discrimination, or unfair labor practices. (See Chapter 3 for more information on the dangers of adopting a rule that isn't consistently enforced.) The better practice, as is true of email, is to allow some personal use of IM. The sample policy language below echoes the personal use policy for email from Chapter 3.

Personal Use of IM

The IM system is intended for official Company business. Although you may send occasional personal instant messages, you may do so during nonwork hours only. If you send personal messages through the Company's IM system, you must exercise discretion as to the number and type of messages you send. You must also ensure that your personal use of IM does not interfere in any way with your job duties or performance. Any employee who abuses this privilege may be subject to discipline.

Lessons From the Real World

Instant messages on employee's work computer lead to search of home computer.

Brian Toon was the vice president of technology solutions at Quotient Inc. until October 31, 2005. In December 2005, Quotient sued Toon for breach of contract and interference with contractual relations, among other things. Quotient claimed that Toon allowed a former Quotient employee access to Quotient's computer system, trade secrets, and other proprietary information, so the former employee could compete against Quotient.

Almost immediately after filing the lawsuit, Quotient asked the judge to allow it to copy the contents of Toon's home computer. Quotient argued that it had discovered evidence on Toon's work computer, including instant messages in which Toon and the former employee discussed competing against Quotient. Quotient also claimed that it had discovered emails and IMs indicating that Toon was using his personal email account and home computer for similar discussions. Quotient asked the court to allow an expert to copy the contents of Toon's home computer, to make sure that no evidence was inadvertently destroyed or overwritten before the court could decide whether Toon would have to hand it over.

Toon opposed the motion, claiming that copying his home computer would invade his and his wife's privacy. Despite this argument, the court allowed his computer to be copied but not reviewed. If the court later determined that Quotient was entitled to view any of the contents, they could be reviewed by Toon's lawyer, so any private, privileged, or otherwise unrelated material could be withheld.

Quotient Inc v. Toon, Case No. 13-C-05-64087 (Md. Cir. Ct. 2005).

Privacy and IM Monitoring

Like your email policy, your IM policy must inform employees that their instant messages are not private, and it must reserve the company's right to monitor and read IMs at any time. Even if your company doesn't currently read employee IM, it may one day have to do so if an employee is accused of sending sexually harassing messages, transmitting trade secrets to a competitor, or using IM to spread false rumors about another employee, for example.

As discussed in Chapter 3, the key to successfully defending against an employee's invasion of privacy claim is to tell employees explicitly that their messages are not private. This is especially important in the context of IM, which seems so ephemeral. (Once the dialog box disappears from the screen, many employees mistakenly assume that it's gone forever and, therefore, can't be retrieved or read by their employer.) Knowing that IM will be read also provides a powerful deterrent to inappropriate content.

What your policy should say about monitoring depends on how your monitoring software works. If, for example, your company uses "keylogger" software that tracks everything an employee types, you should put that information in your policy. If your company uses gateway software that scans outgoing IM for questionable content, you should add that to your policy. You can find sample monitoring policy language in Chapter 3.

RELATED TOPIC

Deciding whether to regularly monitor employee communications can be a very tough call. This is especially true for companies that have positioned themselves, internally or externally, as creative, pro-employee, or simply as a "fun" place to work. For information on the pros and cons of monitoring, see Chapter 3.

IM Is Not Private

Instant messages sent and received on Company equipment are the property of the Company. We reserve the right to access, monitor, read, and/or copy instant messages at any time, for any reason. You should not expect that IMs you send using Company equipment—including messages that you consider to be, or label as, personal—will be private.

Lessons From the Real World

Employee's IM might be private if employer said it wouldn't read the messages.

Jeff Quon was a sergeant on the SWAT team of Ontario, California. He received a pager with wireless text-messaging capability for work, and was told that the department's email policy applied to use of the pagers. That policy said that personal use was a significant policy violation; that the city had the right to monitor all activity; that users should not expect privacy; and that obscene or suggestive messages were prohibited.

However, there was also an informal policy that applied to the pagers. The lieutenant in charge of administering employee use of the pagers told employees that each pager was allotted 25,000 characters per month, and that he would not audit their pagers as long as they paid any overage charges each month. The department did not audit anyone's pager messages for the first eight months after the pagers were issued.

Quon exceeded the character limit three or four times, and paid the overage each time. When Quon and another officer again went over the limit, the chief decided that the messages sent and received on certain pagers (including Quon's) should be audited to figure out whether the city should increase the number of allowed characters and whether the officers were using the pagers for personal reasons. Because the city could not access the messages themselves, it asked its carrier (Arch Wireless) to provide transcripts. Those transcripts revealed that many of Quon's messages were personal and some were sexually explicit. Quon, his wife, and two other people with whom he exchanged text messages sued for violation of their rights to privacy.

The 9th Circuit Court of Appeals found in Quon's favor, ruling that the city had violated his reasonable expectation of privacy. The U.S. Supreme Court did not agree, however. The Supreme Court found that, even if Quon had a reasonable expectation of privacy, the decision to read his text messages was justified. In the Supreme Court's view, that decision had a legitimate, work-related goal—to determine whether the city need to change the character limit on its pagers—and was not excessive in scope, in that the city audited only two months' worth of messages and did not read any messages that had been sent outside of work hours.

Quon v. Arch Wireless Operating Co., 130 S.Ct. 2619 (2010).

Inappropriate Content Rules

As email and IM have become more popular, they have also become vehicles for inappropriate conduct. The potential content problems your company might encounter in IM are essentially the same as it might find in email: harassment, inappropriate jokes and comments, solicitations for various causes or businesses, lack of professionalism, and so on. In fact, the extremely informal nature of IM makes it even more vulnerable to these types of problems.

If your company has adopted IM in some form, then you should make clear that your company's conduct rules apply with full force to IM.

Lessons From the Real World

Employee fired for IM message claims that he was reporting harassment.

Todd Bernier was fired from his job as an equities analyst at Morningstar, Inc., for sending an instant message to a coworker, Christopher Davis. Bernier felt that Davis, who is gay, had sexually harassed him by staring at his private parts while both were using the urinal. (During the litigation, it came out that Davis has a "lazy eye" that sometimes makes it appear that he's looking at something else while conversing.) Rather than using the company's harassment complaint process, Bernier sent an anonymous IM to Davis through the company's internal system, saying "Stop staring! The guys on the floor don't like it."

Unlike Bernier, Davis did use the company's complaint process—to claim that he had been sexually harassed. The company investigated. When questioned, Bernier denied sending the IM; he was fired several hours later. At the termination meeting, Bernier admitted sending the IM and explained why he did so. Bernier later sued Morningstar for sexual harassment and retaliation.

Bernier lost on both claims. The court found no evidence that the company knew he was claiming harassment. He didn't use the company's complaint process, sent the IM anonymously to a coworker, and then denied sending it. Even after Davis brought the IM to the company's attention, there was no reason for the company to infer that the sender of the IM—as opposed to the recipient—felt sexually harassed.

Bernier v. Morningstar, Inc., 495 F.3d 369 (7th Cir. 2007).

All Conduct Rules Apply to IM

All of our policies and rules of conduct apply to employee use of instant messaging (IM). This means, for example, that you may not use IM to send harassing or discriminatory messages, including messages with explicit sexual content or pornographic images; to send threatening messages; or to reveal Company trade secrets.

Viruses and Security Threats

IM can be especially vulnerable to viruses, worms, and bots because of the way these threats travel. Unlike spam, which often has a nonsensical subject line and is sent from an unknown source, IM malware looks like an actual message from someone known to the recipient. Once an IM security threat infects one person's account, it typically sends itself to everyone on that person's buddy list within hours. A buddy who opens the message or downloads an attached file then becomes the next infectious agent. If you have permitted IM in your company, you should adopt the policy below.

IM Security

To avoid viruses and other threats, employees should not open instant messages or file attachments from people and businesses they don't recognize. Even if you know the sender, do not open an IM attachment that has a strange name or is not referenced in the body of the IM—it may have been transmitted automatically, without the sender's knowledge.

If you believe your computer has been infected by a virus, worm, or other security threat to the Company's system, you must inform the IT department immediately.

Employees may not share their IM password with anyone, nor may they use another employee's IM account.

Retention and Deletion

Like email messages, instant messages are electronic records. This means not only that your company may have a need, or an obligation, to retain some of these records, but also that these documents may be subject to discovery in a lawsuit. IMs are probably less likely to contain important information that your company needs to keep, simply because instant messaging doesn't lend itself to formal correspondence (for example, job applications, contract negotiations, or performance feedback). Most IMs your company generates can safely be deleted once the conversation ends.

For those few IMs that may have to be retained, your policy should explain how employees can save them. (And, at the same time, your company should institute training procedures so that employees understand how to retain and archive such messages.) It should also explain that other IMs—those that the company isn't obligated to keep—should be deleted once they are dealt with.

Retaining and Deleting Instant Messages

Because instant messages are electronic records, certain IMs must be retained for compliance purposes. Please refer to our record-keeping policy for guidance on which records must be kept, and for how long. If you have any questions about whether and how to retain a particular IM, please ask your manager.

We discourage employees from storing instant messages that are not subject to the retention rules explained above. Please make a regular practice of deleting IMs once you have read and/or responded to them. If you need to save a particular message, you may print out a paper copy, archive the message, or save it on your hard drive or disk. The Company will purge IMs that have not been archived after _____ days.

Some IM Slang—HTH!

Emails, text messaging, and IMs, have helped to create a new slanguage with terms such as LOL (laughing out loud) or BFF (best friends forever). Many of these terms are simple acronyms; some use the sound of letters and numbers to create words (such as L8R for "later" or NE1 for "anyone"). Here are some of the more common (that don't include curse words):

AFAIK: as far as I know

AFK: away from keyboard

BTDT: been there, done that

CU: see you

EOM: end of message

FWIW: for what it's worth

HAND: have a nice day

HTH: hope this/that helps

IANAL: I am not a lawyer

IMHO: in my humble opinion

IYKWIM: if you know what I mean

j/k: just kidding

MYOB: mind your own business

NSFW: not safe for work

OMG: oh my god

OTOH: on the other hand

SCNR: sorry, could not resist

TBH: to be honest

TMI: too much information

TTFN: ta ta for now

WRT: with respect to

YW: you're welcome

CAUTION

Don't forget the acknowledgment form. If your company adopts the instant messaging policy covered in this chapter, make sure you require employees to sign an acknowledgment form. You'll find a sample acknowledgment form and instructions in at this book's companion page at Nolo's website; see the appendix for more information.

Putting It All Together: A Sample Instant Messaging Policy

Here's a sample IM policy adopted by a company with a large sales force. The company decides to allow use of consumer IM to facilitate communication between salespeople and their customers. Salespeople are paid on commission, so the company isn't too worried about them wasting time on personal IM. As a result, it has decided not to monitor IM, but only to reserve its right to do so.

Instant Messaging Policy

Using Consumer Instant Messaging Software

Our Company makes instant messaging (IM) capability available to our employees. If you wish to use IM, you must notify the IT department and let them know which publicly available IM software you would like to use. The IT department will download the appropriate software and set up your IM account.

Employees may not download or use any IM software on their own, without going through the IT department. Violation of this policy will result in discipline, up to and including termination.

IM Usernames and Passwords

Employees will be assigned an IM user ID and password by the IT department. Employees may not change their user ID without permission.

If you have a personal account with any IM software provider, you may not use Company equipment to access your personal account. You may use only the ID and password provided by the Company.

Personal Use of IM

The IM system is intended for official Company business. Although you may send occasional personal instant messages, you may do so during nonwork hours only. If you send personal messages through the Company's IM system, you must exercise discretion as to the number and type of messages you send. You must also ensure that your personal use of IM does not interfere in any way with your job duties or performance. Any employee who abuses this privilege may be subject to discipline.

IM Is Not Private

Instant messages sent and received on Company equipment are the property of the Company. We reserve the right to access, monitor, read, and/or copy instant messages at any time, for any reason. You should not expect that IM you send using Company equipment— including messages that you consider to be, or label as, personal—will be private.

All Conduct Rules Apply to IM

All of our policies and rules of conduct apply to employee use of instant messaging (IM). This means, for example, that you may not use IM to send harassing or discriminatory messages, including messages with explicit sexual content or pornographic images; to send threatening messages; or to reveal Company trade secrets.

IM Security

To avoid viruses and other threats, employees should not open instant messages or file attachments from people and businesses they don't recognize. Even if you know the sender, do not open an IM attachment that has a strange name or is not referenced in the body of the IM— it may have been transmitted automatically, without the sender's knowledge.

If you believe your computer has been infected by a virus, worm, or other security threat to the Company's system, you must inform the IT department immediately.

Employees may not share their IM password with anyone, nor may they use another employee's IM account.

Retaining and Deleting Instant Messages

Because instant messages are electronic records, certain IMs must be retained for compliance purposes. Please refer to our record-keeping policy for guidance on which records must be kept, and for how long. If you have any questions about whether and how to retain a particular IM, please ask your manager.

We discourage employees from storing instant messages that are not subject to the retention rules explained above. Please make a regular practice of deleting IMs once you have read and/or responded to them. If you need to save a particular message, you may print out a paper copy, archive the message, or save it on your hard drive or disk. The Company will purge IMs that have not been archived after 90 days.

Social Media, Blogs, and Beyond: Personal Posting on the Internet

In This Chapter:

Policy Provisions for Blogs and Personal Postings

☐ Personal Blogs and Online Posts

☐ No Posting Using Company Resources

☐ Guidelines for Blogs and Online Posts

Chances are very good that many of your company's employees are posting personal content on the Internet. They may be posting at their own blog or website, or they may be posting at social networking or community sites—for example, uploading photos, adding comments to other websites, sending out tweets, or exchanging parenting advice or recipes in a chat room. In some cases, however, employees may use these avenues for personal expression to vent about coworkers, supervisors, customers, and other workplace issues. And, some may express personal opinions—unrelated to their job—that could harm the company's reputation.

Employers face a dilemma. Most are understandably wary about trying to "crack down" on personal postings. After all, blogs and other personal sites are often a creative outlet, a way for friends and people with similar interests to stay in touch, a place to share opinions and be part of a larger community of Xena fans, pug owners, single parents, or recycling enthusiasts. They are, in a word, personal, and few employers really want to snoop through their employees' personal writings or be known as the company that stifles personal expression.

Unfortunately, however, not all employees like their jobs. An employee blog or Facebook page that reveals company trade secrets, slams a company product that's about to be released, or threatens or harasses other employees can also be an unmitigated disaster for the company. Even posts that have nothing to do with work can create major workplace problems, if they express extreme and unpopular views, racist comments, or violent fantasies, for example. This chapter explains what you can and can't do in regulating employee posts, and provides policy language that gives employees some ground rules for Internet content. For information and policy language on employee posts to company sites or pages, see Chapter 7.

CAUTION
Rules for employee posts—especially on social media sites—are in flux. Recently, the National Labor Relations Board (NLRB), the government agency that regulates labor and union issues, has come down hard on employers with social media policies that might restrict discussion of working conditions. Policy language that many companies have used for years has been struck down as too likely to lead employees to believe that they may not criticize the company's policies and practices online, in violation of the right employees have to freely discuss working conditions with each other. The legal terrain is changing rapidly in this area, so check your social media policy with a lawyer to make sure it complies with the most recent legal decisions.

Restrictions on Personal Posting

As an employer, you have the right to control what employees do with the time and equipment you pay for, generally speaking. When employees use their own computers and devices to express their own opinions on their own time, however, an employer's legal rights are more limited—as is an employer's practical ability to crack down on employee posting, not to mention an employer's incentive to take action that will undoubtedly alienate large numbers of employees.

In this situation, the best offense is a good defense. Your company can manage the potential legal exposure and bad publicity that could result from employee posts that cross the line—without going overboard in policing employee expression—by adopting a policy that lets employees know where the line is. This section explains some legal rules and practical considerations to keep in mind as you review your options.

CAUTION

If access to an employee site is restricted, don't go there. If an employee restricts access to a blog or website, an employer who breaks into the site can get into trouble. That's what happened when the vice president of Hawaiian Airlines used an employee's name and password to access a private website created by a Hawaiian pilot, where the pilot and other authorized visitors posted bulletins critical of the airline, its officers, and the pilots' union. The 9th Circuit Court of Appeals allowed the site's owner to go forward with his lawsuit against Hawaiian for violating the Stored Communications Act. (*Konop v. Hawaiian Airlines*, 302 F.3d 868 (9th Cir. 2002).) A federal district court in New Jersey reached the same conclusion in upholding a jury award for employees who were fired after a manager accessed an invitation-only Myspace page where employees vented about the company; the manager allegedly pressured an employee to give up her user name and password to access the site. *Pietrylo v. Hillstone Restaurant Group*, 2009 WL 3128420 (D. N.J. 2009).

Legal Protections for Employees Who Post Online

Not surprisingly, there are a host of laws that protect an employee's right to speak freely online. Here's a rundown:

- **Off-duty conduct laws.** A number of states have passed laws that prohibit employers from disciplining or firing employees for activities they pursue off-site, on their own time. Although some of these laws were originally intended to protect smokers from discrimination—they tend to include language protecting employees who "use legal products" while off duty—others protect any employee conduct that doesn't break the law. These laws could provide legal protection for an employee who keeps a blog.

- **Protections for political views.** A handful of states protect employees from discrimination based on their political views or affiliation. In these states, disciplining an employee for personal posts that endorse a particular candidate or cause could be illegal.

- **Protections for "whistlebloggers."** An employee who raises concerns about safety hazards or illegal activity at work may be protected as a whistleblower (or a "whistleblogger," if the concerns are raised in a blog). Whistleblower protections recognize that the public good is served by employees who are willing to come forward with these types of complaints—and that very few employees will do so if they can be fired for it.

- **Prohibitions on retaliation.** A variety of employment laws protect employees from retaliation for claiming that their rights have been violated. If an employee's blog post complains of workplace discrimination, harassment, violation of the Family and Medical Leave Act, wage and hour violations, or other legal transgressions, that employee may be protected from disciplinary action.

 TIP
The First Amendment doesn't apply in private employment. Many employees mistakenly believe that the right to free speech and freedom of the press, enshrined in the First Amendment of the U.S. Constitution, protects their right to say or write whatever they want online, in a blog or otherwise. However, the Constitution only protects individual rights as against government intrusion, not against private companies. If a state government tried to ban what private citizens could say on their blogs, that would raise a First Amendment issue. If the government isn't involved, however, the First Amendment doesn't come into play.

These days, the most likely enforcer of employee rights online is the National Labor Relations Board (NLRB), the government agency that investigates and enforces the nation's labor and union laws. What do employee posts have to do with labor relations? Plenty, if employees are fired or disciplined for (or prohibited by policy from) communicating with each other about the terms and conditions of employment and joining together to bring their concerns to their employer. Employees enjoy these rights to communicate with each other and raise group concerns to their employer (called "protected concerted activity" or simply "Section 7 activity," after the provision of the National Labor Relations Act which creates them) whether or not they are represented by a union.

In the last few years, the NLRB has become extremely active in going after employers who fire or discipline employees for posting critical comments about the company on social media sites or blogs. (You can find several NLRB reports on these cases at its website, www.nlrb.gov.) For example:

- A collections agency was found to have illegally fired an employee for Facebook posts complaining about her transfer. The employee used expletives and said she was done with being a good employee; her coworkers who were Facebook friends posted comments expressing support, criticizing the employer, and suggesting a class action lawsuit. Because the employees were discussing taking action regarding the terms of their employment, the NLRB concluded that they were engaged in protected concerted activity.

- An employee at a veterinary hospital posted to her Facebook page after being denied a promotion. Several coworkers responded to the post, and engaged in a conversation in which they complained about the person who received the promotion, the company's practices regarding raises and reviews, and so on. The NLRB found it illegal when the employee and one friend were fired, and the other two participants in the conversation disciplined.

- A group of employees took to Facebook to complain about a coworker who they felt had been criticizing their performance. A conversation about the employer's policies towards its clientele ensued, then five of the employees were fired. The NLRB found the firings illegal, because the employees were discussing the terms of their employment and considering how to raise those concerns with their employer.

As part of these enforcement actions, the NLRB often finds that the employer's social media and posting policy is too broad, because it would tend to discourage employees from exercising their right to engage in Section 7 activity. The Board has objected to policies that prohibit disparagement or criticism of others; policies that require employees not to post "confidential" or "non-public" information (unless the policy illustrates the types of information covered, so as not to dissuade employees from discussing wages or other terms of employment); policies that require employees to avoid picking fights or discussing topics that are objectionable or inflammatory; and policies that require employees to check with a supervisor before posting.

Don't Ask Employees For Their Social Media Passwords

Many companies look online for publicly available information on job or promotion applicants, including on Facebook and other social networking sites. But the Maryland Department of Corrections took this common practice a step further when it asked employee Robert Collins to hand over his Facebook password during a job recertification interview.

The situation was publicized when the American Civil Liberties Union filed a lawsuit on Collins' behalf in 2011. Soon after, Maryland passed a law banning this practice, and Illinois followed suit. Several other states are considering similar legislation; check the website of the National Conference of State Legislatures, www.ncsl.org, for up-to-date information.

Practical Concerns When Limiting Personal Posts

In addition to legal concerns, there are also practical reasons why your company should tread carefully when seeking to regulate personal blogs and online posts.

- **The "POS" factor.** Children on the Internet often use the acronym POS (for "parent over shoulder") to indicate that they can't speak freely because a parent has entered the room. Employees are very likely to see your company restrictions on personal posting at home in the same way—overly restrictive and unnecessarily intrusive. Why should an employer care whether employees post about their kitchen remodel, their children's health problems, or their favorite band? The more a company tries to limit what its employees do off duty, the more employees are likely to feel like prisoners or children, rather than valued members of a team.

- **Public relations concerns.** An employer that tries to prohibit or greatly restrict personal posting also runs into a potential public relations problem: The online community doesn't like— and will publicize—efforts to silence one of their ranks. The result could be a blog swarm or a Twit storm of bad PR for your company.

- **Enforcement problems.** It can be tough to enforce a restrictive policy on employee posts. If they post from home, how will you find out about it? Are you really going to dedicate human resources to finding and reading employee blogs and Facebook pages? If an employee uses a pseudonym (as most bloggers do) and doesn't name your company or other employees, how are you going to know about the blog or page? How much time and effort is your company willing to put into policing employees' personal posts? For most companies, the answer is not much (if any).

Lessons From the Real World

Lockheed employee blows the whistle on YouTube.

Michael De Kort, an engineer at Lockheed Martin, was concerned about design flaws in work the company was doing to refurbish patrol boats for the Coast Guard. The flaws included blind spots in the boats' surveillance systems, security problems with the communications systems, and possible equipment malfunction in cold weather.

De Kort spoke to his supervisors, government investigators, and even members of Congress. He felt his concerns weren't being taken seriously, so he posted a video of himself talking about them on YouTube. Six months later, a government report confirmed some of his complaints. And, in January 2008, he received an award from the Society of Social Implications of Technology, for "high ethical standards in protecting or promoting the interests and safety of the public." Lockheed apparently didn't share the love for De Kort: He was fired shortly after posting the video, for what Lockheed said were cost-cutting reasons.

Adopting a Commonsense Policy

Online postings are easy to dash off and virtually impossible to retract once published. When employees aren't at work, they probably aren't thinking of the potential consequences of making fun of a coworker's accent or revealing little-known facts about a client. Most likely, they're simply trying to be funny and attract readers.

What can your company do to curb inappropriate employee posts without going overboard? Adopt a policy letting employees know that their personal blogs could get them in trouble at work, and explain what types of content could be problematic.

Having a written policy on personal posts puts employees on notice that their personal writings could get them into professional trouble (something that many employees seem not to fully understand). In short, it may remind them to think before they publish posts that cross the line.

Blogs About Work: More Positive Than You Might Think

Most employers fear an employee blog or post that slams a company product, makes fun of coworkers, or otherwise shows the company in a bad light. Believe it or not, however, some research shows that employees who blog about work are fairly positive about their jobs. In the first six months of 2005, Edelman and Intelliseek tracked blogs for mentions of "love my job," "hate work," and "hate my boss," and found that "love my job" came up twice as often as "hate work," and four times as often as "hate my boss." You can find more results at Edelman's website, www.edelman.com; select "Insights," then "Talking From the Inside Out: The Rise of Employee Bloggers" (2005).

To start your company's policy, you'll want to assure employees that the company supports their personal creative efforts, while also reminding them that discussing work on a personal blog can lead to problems.

Personal Blogs and Online Posts

Our Company recognizes that some of our employees may choose to express themselves by posting personal information on the Internet through personal websites, social media, blogs, or chat rooms, by uploading content, or by making comments at other websites or blogs. We value our employees' creativity and honor your interest in engaging in these forms of personal expression on your own time, should you choose to do so.

However, problems can arise when a personal posting identifies or appears to be associated with our Company, or when a personal posting is used in ways that violate the Company's rights or the rights of other employees.

No Posting Using Company Resources

Your policy should prohibit employees from using the company's computer systems to write or publish personal posts. While you might think few employees would blog from work, you'd be wrong: According to the Pew Project's 2006 report, 7% of bloggers "usually" blog from work, and another 6% blog from both home and work. Although these aren't the highest percentages, they're out of tens of millions who keep blogs, which adds up to a lot of lost work hours.

Social Media Freedom More Important Than Salary to Generation Z

In 2011, Cisco surveyed more than 2,800 college students and young professionals in 14 countries—the so-called "millenials" or Generation Z. Given the generally crummy state of the economy, it seemed logical that those who were looking for jobs (or soon to be) would list their primary concerns as, well, just whether they'd be able to find work, along with salary, salary, and salary.

But no. According to this survey, it's all about social networking, portable electronic devices, and working from home or other remote locations. Here are a few choice bits:

More than half said that if their company banned access to social media sites from work, they would either turn down a job offer or find a way to get around the prohibition.

40% of college students—and 45% of young professionals—said they would accept lower paying work if it offered more flexibility regarding social media access, mobility, and device choice.

About 70% said they should be allowed to access personal sites and social media sites using company-owned devices.

No Posting Using Company Resources

You may not use Company resources to create or maintain a personal blog, personal website, or personal page on a social networking site, or to upload content or make personal postings online, nor may you do so on Company time.

Ground Rules for Posting Content

Your company's policy should give employees some guidelines for posting online, whether to personal blogs, personal websites, social media, or community sites. Your goal here is to make sure employees know that they post at their own risk. Many employees don't realize that they can get into personal legal trouble for what they post. Despite a handful of well-publicized firings based on employee posts, some employees still don't realize that writing about work can lead to the unemployment line.

By making sure employees know the risks, and setting down some ground rules for posts that deal with your company, your policy can encourage employees to stop and think before they hit "publish." At the same time, your policy must not discourage employees from sharing concerns—and even complaints—about working conditions, pay, and so on with coworkers.

Fired for Online Posting

Are you wondering how far an employee has to go to get fired for posting information or opinions on the Internet? Of course, it all depends on your company's philosophy, the employee's disciplinary history, how much damage the employee's post actually causes, and many other factors. Here are some real-world examples of posts that have led to termination, along with links to the blogs or news coverage of them:

- Heather Armstrong was fired by her employer (whom she never identified on her blog) for humorous posts about annoying habits of her coworkers and company management, what she actually did when she was supposed to be working at home, and other things. Her website, www.dooce.com, brought the word "dooced" to the modern lexicon (it means to get fired for blogging).

- Two employees of Domino's pizza were fired after they posted a YouTube video in which one of them put cheese up his nose before putting it on a sandwich; they were also hit with felony charges (www.nytimes.com/2009/04/16/business/media/16dominos.html).

- A British travel agent was fired after complaining about a coworker on Facebook, saying "I swear I will smack the brown-nosing cow in the face before the end of my shift!" (www.mirror.co.uk/news/top-stories/2010/03/19/travel-agent-fired-over-facebook-cow-jibe-115875-22122628).

- Matt Donegan, a reporter and editor, was fired by *The Dover Post* after his MySpace blog included an entry that complained about his African-American neighbors partying late into the night and speculated whether similar circumstances might have led to the assassination of Martin Luther King, Jr. Donegan said the post was intended as a joke. His employer was not LOL (www.nbc10.com/news/6667658/detail.html).

Guidelines for Online Posting

You are legally responsible for content you post to the Internet, in a blog, social media site, or otherwise. You can be held personally liable for defaming others, revealing trade secrets, and copyright infringement, among other things.

All of our Company policies apply to anything you write in a personal blog, post to the Internet, or upload to the Internet. This means, for example, that you may not use personal postings to harass or threaten other employees or reveal Company trade secrets or confidential information, such as internal reports or confidential company communications.

If, in the process of making a personal post or upload on the Internet, you identify yourself as an employee of our Company, whether by explicit statement or by implication, you must clearly state that the views expressed in your post, or at your blog, social media page, or website, are your own, and do not reflect the views of the Company.

You may not use the Company's trademarks, logos, copyrighted material, branding, or other intellectual property in a way that violates intellectual property law.

The Company may have a legal duty not to disclose certain facts, such as information on stock offerings. Employees much follow the law and refrain from making any prohibited financial disclosures.

Please keep in mind that your personal postings will be read not only by your friends and family, but possibly by your coworkers and bosses, as well as our Company's customers, clients, and competitors. Even if you post anonymously or under a pseudonym, your identity can be discovered relatively easily. Use your common sense when deciding what to include in a post or comment. Don't say something that you wouldn't want these people to read.

Rules for Endorsements

Does your company sell its products on sites that allow users to comment or review the products, such as Amazon? Does your company appear on online review sites, such as Yelp? Are your company's products discussed in user boards, blogs, and/or social networking sites? If so, you need to make sure that employees always identify themselves—and their relationship to your company—if they post content or reviews of your company's products. In fact, it's a good idea to require employees to identify themselves in any post about the company to avoid the possibility of misleading readers.

Is That You, Rahodeb?

Whole Foods cofounder John Mackey posted more than 1,000 entries on Yahoo Finance's online bulletin board over seven years, under the name "Rahodeb" (a mashup of his wife's name, Deborah). He wrote a lot about Whole Foods, expressed some negative opinions about rival (and acquisition target) Wild Oats, and on occasion paid himself anonymous compliments, such as "I like Mackey's haircut. I think he looks cute!" Mackey finally revealed his true identity online, after losing a bet.

Andrew Martin, "Whole Foods Executive Used Alias," *New York Times*, July 12, 2007.

In 2009, the Federal Trade Commission (FTC), the federal government agency that regulates deceptive advertising and other consumer protection matters, issued regulations governing endorsements and testimonials about products, including statements that appear online. The purpose of these rules is to make sure consumers fully understand the relationship between the person making the endorsement and the product, so they can make informed decisions about how much weight to give the endorser's statement. A statement by an actor or a paid spokesperson probably isn't as credible as a statement by an actual user of the product, for example. The FTC rules seek to make the relationship between the product and the person raving about it explicit.

What do these rules have to do with employee posts? If employees post anything about your company's products online, they must identify themselves as employees of the company. The FTC has said that an employment relationship is the type of connection that a consumer would want to know about in evaluating product endorsements. (The FTC gives the example of an employee secretly promoting the company's playback devices at an online message board for enthusiasts of music download technology.) So, your policy must tell employees that if they post reviews or other types of statements about company products, they must be up front about their relationship to the company.

Promoting the Company or Its Products or Services

Do not engage in covert marketing or endorsements for the Company or its products or services. If you post anything about the Company, you must identify yourself as a Company employee. You are legally required to identify your employment relationship if it might be relevant to a consumer's decision to patronize our company or your failure to do so could be misleading to readers. This means, for example, that employees may not post anonymous online reviews of Company products or promotional statements about the Company in which they fail to identify themselves as employees.

Espresso Addict, Indeed: Company Employee Posts 12 Product Reviews

As reported on his own blog and the *Wall Street Journal* blog, Russ Taylor was shopping for an espresso machine. He was reading Amazon reviews of high-end coffee products when he noticed that someone named "T. Carpenter" had written 12 reviews, all giving five stars to products made by DeLonghi. In fact, he noticed that the ubiquitous reviewer had submitted one review that said "instead of buying two different machines for my family I bough[t] only this DeLonghi machine," yet had posted a separate review of a different espresso maker the same day.

Smelling a rat, Taylor did a Google search and found that someone named Tara Carpenter worked as a communications manager for DeLonghi. Taylor got in touch with DeLonghi, but received no substantive response. That changed when Taylor passed the news item on to the *Wall Street Journal*. DeLonghi took that phone call, and confirmed to the *Journal* that Carpenter worked for the company and posted the reviews. In its defense, DeLonghi pointed out that it saw no false statements in the reviews, and that its employees "are passionate about the products we make and sell." Indeed.

Friending at Work

Socializing among coworkers doesn't just take place during coffee breaks, lunch, and after-work happy hours any more. Now, coworkers can also keep up with each other's romances, family outings, candid photos, and daily doings online, too, by "friending" each other on Facebook, following each other on Twitter, or otherwise joining each other's online social networks.

Unfortunately, what many see as good clean fun can quickly become a workplace problem. What if one coworker is left out of the network and feels excluded from the team? What if a manager posts photos of himself at a rally opposing gay marriage—and a gay subordinate starts to wonder if his sexual orientation is preventing him from getting promoted? What if a manager sends a friend request to a subordinate who really doesn't want to reciprocate, but feels she can't turn down her manager? Social media create many opportunities to blur the line between work lives and private lives, sometimes with unprofessional and unkind results.

Some companies prohibit managers from friending subordinates, period. There are legal reasons why such a restrictive policy makes sense, if the subordinate ever has a gripe with the supervisor or the company. In that situation, the subordinate (or his or her lawyer, in the worst case scenario) could sift through every post the manager has made, looking for evidence of discriminatory beliefs, inappropriate behavior, illegal or unprofessional goings on inside the company, and so on.

At the same time, however, a policy this restrictive will almost certainly meet with tremendous resistance. After all, it tells employees whom they may communicate with on their own time, using their own equipment. Also, this type of policy would be very difficult to enforce. While a cost-benefit analysis might convince some companies to adopt restrictions like these, most won't want to go this far in dictating employee behavior off the job.

The sensible middle ground here is to alert employees to the problem and ask them to use discretion when social networking with work colleagues.

Social Networking With Colleagues

Use your good judgment when requesting that coworkers, managers, or subordinates join your online social networks, or when responding to such requests. The Company does not tolerate conduct or communications toward work colleagues that violate company policy—such as sexual harassment, bullying, threats—whether they take place online or off.

CAUTION

Don't forget the acknowledgment form. If your company adopts the personal blogs and online posting policy covered in this chapter, make sure you require employees to sign an acknowledgment form. You'll find a sample acknowledgment form and instructions at this book's companion page at www.nolo.com; see the appendix for more information.

Putting It All Together: A Sample Blog and Personal Post Policy

Here's a sample blog and personal post policy adopted by a company that designs software. The company encourages employee creativity and independent thinking, so it doesn't want to be seen as banning employees' personal expression. Many of its employees keep their own blogs and post to a variety of online forums, however, so the company decides that it needs to establish guidelines.

Personal Blogs and Online Posts

Our Company recognizes that some of our employees may choose to express themselves by posting personal information on the Internet through personal websites, social media, blogs, or chat rooms, by uploading content, or by making comments at other websites or blogs. We value our employees' creativity and honor your interest in engaging in these forms of personal expression on your own time, should you choose to do so.

However, problems can arise when a personal posting identifies or appears to be associated with our Company, or when a personal posting is used in ways that violate the Company's rights or the rights of other employees.

No Posting Using Company Resources

You may not use Company resources to create or maintain a personal blog, personal website, or personal page on a social networking site, or to upload content or make personal postings online, nor may you do so on Company time.

Guidelines for Online Posting

You are legally responsible for content you post to the Internet, in a blog, social media site, or otherwise. You can be held personally liable for defaming others, revealing trade secrets, and copyright infringement, among other things.

All of our Company policies apply to anything you write in a personal blog, post to the Internet, or upload to the Internet. This means, for example, that you may not use personal postings to harass or threaten other employees or reveal Company trade secrets or confidential information, such as internal reports or confidential company communications.

If, in the process of making a personal post or upload on the Internet, you identify yourself as an employee of our Company, whether by explicit statement or by implication, you must clearly state that the views expressed in your post, or at your blog, social media page, or website, are your own, and do not reflect the views of the Company.

You may not use the Company's trademarks, logos, copyrighted material, branding, or other intellectual property in a way that violates intellectual property law.

The Company may have a legal duty not to disclose certain facts, such as information on stock offerings. Employees must follow the law and refrain from making any prohibited financial disclosures.

Please keep in mind that your personal postings will be read not only by your friends and family, but possibly by your coworkers and bosses, as well as our Company's customers, clients, and competitors. Even if you post anonymously or under a pseudonym, your identity can be discovered relatively easily. Use your common sense when deciding what to include in a post or comment. Don't say something that you wouldn't want these people to read.

Promoting the Company or Its Products or Services

Do not engage in covert marketing or endorsements for the Company or its products or services. If you post anything about the Company, you must identify yourself as a Company employee. You are legally required to identify your employment relationship if it might be relevant to a consumer's decision to patronize our company or your failure to do so could be misleading to readers. This means, for example, that employees may not post anonymous online reviews of Company products or promotional statements about the Company in which they fail to identify themselves as employees.

Social Networking With Colleagues

Use your good judgment when requesting that coworkers, managers, or subordinates join your online social networks, or when responding to such requests. The Company does not tolerate conduct or communications toward work colleagues that violate company policies—such as sexual harassment, bullying, or threats—whether they take place online or off.

Company-Sponsored Social Media

In This Chapter:

Policy Provisions for Company-Sponsored Social Media

☐ Our Company's Social Media Presence

☐ Who May Post

☐ Guidelines for Employees Who Post

☐ Authorship and Disclaimers

☐ Handling Comments

D oes your company have a business blog, pages on social networking sites (like Facebook or LinkedIn), a Twitter feed, or a YouTube channel? If so, you're in good company. These days, it's the rare business that doesn't have some presence in social media. These tools offer great opportunities to market a company and its products, to reach consumers and potential employees, and to position the company as a player in the field. Visibility on the Web—particularly in the places where coveted customers socialize, research products, and shop—can translate directly into increased brand loyalty and higher revenues.

Sounds great, right? But it doesn't happen by itself. Somebody has to write all those posts, comments, and tweets for your company's social media pages—and the people your company taps to handle these online communications must have some guidance on acceptable and unacceptable content. Otherwise, they could unknowingly fall into the traps for unwary bloggers and posters discussed in Chapter 6, from defamation and copyright claims to invasion of privacy, disclosure of trade secrets, and public relations disasters. Only this time, your company will share the liability—and suffer most of the harm—for inappropriate or illegal employee posts.

RELATED TOPIC

For policy language and information on employees' personal posts, see Chapter 6. This chapter covers the company's online content: the social media posts employees write for the company as part of their jobs. Personal posts—such as an employee's own Facebook page, YouTube videos, or blog feeds—are covered in Chapter 6.

The employees who handle your company's social media presence need clear guidelines. The success of social media is based on attracting the most viewers through immediate interaction. Because social media places a premium on fresh information (as well as the humorous, clever, and hip), there is often a temptation to resort to the lowest common denominators in order to achieve viral success. Employees may, for example, be tempted to cross the lines from edgy humor into bad taste; or to create a news scoop by leaking a company secret. This chapter provides policy language that will help your employees understand how to stay on the right side of the line when posting to your company's social media pages.

How the Fortune 500 Use Social Media

According to recent statistics, the Fortune 500 is adopting social media at a rapid clip:

- Almost a quarter of the companies have a public blog.
- 35% have a live Twitter account (one that had at least one post in the previous month).
- 31% have incorporated online video into their websites.
- 19% are podcasting.

("The Fortune 500 and Social Media: A Longitudinal Study of Blogging and Twitter Usage by America's Largest Companies," available at the website of the Society for New Communications Research, http://sncr.org.)

Which social media are the most popular among the most successful companies? Of the Fortune 100, a 2010 survey showed that 65% have Twitter accounts, 54% have a Facebook page, and 50% have a YouTube channel. ("Burston-Marsteller Fortune Global 100 Social Media Study," available at www.burston-marsteller.com.) And executives from all of the Fortune 500 companies maintain accounts at LinkedIn (www.linkedin.com).

Why Post?

A lot of attempts at social media quickly peter out. Statistics show that many company blogs expire from lack of interest, corporate Facebook fan pages become inactive, and Twitter feeds dissolve into the vapors. One of the main reasons for these failures is that so many companies jumped on the Web 2.0 bandwagon because it was "the next big thing," without giving much thought to what they hoped to accomplish with their blog or social networking page. The result for many companies was a series of glorified public relations posts that did not provide any real value to customers and, therefore, didn't attract much of a following.

What makes social media unique is that it is an interactive, constantly changing medium: Unlike a regular website, which generally provides static information, social networking tools facilitate communication. The result may be a two-way conversation, as when a customer posts a comment on your company's Facebook page, then your company responds, directly or online. Or, it could be a much larger discussion. If a new regulation affects your industry, for example, your in-house expert might write about it on the company's blog, citing to other experts who have weighed in and news articles on the topic. Your blog may then be cited by other blogs and news articles in turn, creating an ongoing conversation that can be followed by anyone who's interested. This type of communication generates media hits for your company, boosts your search engine optimization (SEO), shows that you are up on important issues in your industry, and brings in more readers (some of whom will, hopefully, turn into customers).

The purpose of engaging social media for most companies is twofold: to promote your business and to provide value to consumers. But how do you want to do that? Is it by providing "name that donut?" Twitter feeds à la Dunkin' Donuts? Is it by showing off otherwise unknown software product features à la Adobe blogs? Is it by dazzling readers with design, Web culture, and usability information as pioneered by the wildly successful corporate blog, Signal v. Noise, from 37Signals.com?

Whatever your plans include, if you're asking employees to represent your company online and to be its written voice and public face, it's only fair to tell them what you want them to do in that capacity. In other words, you should start your policy only *after* you've given some thought to where your company wants to be online and what you want to accomplish there.

That will depend on many variables, including your field, your products or services, your customer base, your resources, and more.

The introductory language provided below will work for many companies that want to use social media to market and publicize the company and its products.

Our Company's Social Media Presence

Social media tools, including Company-sponsored blogs and microblogs, social networking sites, video or picture sharing sites, wikis, and other means of communicating online, are an important part of our Company's face to the public. These social media offer opportunities to shape opinion about our products and our company, to communicate directly with customers and clients, to provide added value for our customers, and to be part of the online conversation about important developments in our field.

If your company has more specific goals in creating or maintaining a social media presence, you should include them at the end of this paragraph. Here are some examples:

Our Company's affiliation with the athletes who use our products is at the heart of our marketing efforts. We hope to build customer interest in our company by featuring the achievements of our sponsored athletes—and offering opportunities for amateur athletes who use our products to join the conversation—in all of our social media efforts.

We want to use social media to educate consumers and to generate interest in our soy-based line of meat replacement products, using content that will appeal to and expand our customer base. This might include things like recipes and information on the health benefits of soy products, vegetarian diets, organic foods, and so on.

> Our social media strategy centers on our connection with the San Francisco Bay Area, where we have been based for more than a century. We want to provide social media content that emphasizes and builds this relationship, such as information about San Francisco history (and our role in it, including helping to rebuild after the 1906 earthquake!), other local businesses, facts and lore about the city, and features on local customers.

Who May Post

Your policy should specify that employees must be authorized to post content to company sites. Some companies—such as those in the fields of high-tech or information services—may decide to allow most employees to post. At other companies, only a select few will have the expertise and savvy to speak for the company. Either way, your policy should explain your method of authorizing employees to represent the company via social media.

Your company should also provide some training for employees who will post on the company's behalf. There are many posting pitfalls for the unwary and your company will likely be responsible for employee posts to official company sites, so it is absolutely vital to train employees who will represent the company online.

> **Who May Post**
>
> Only authorized employees may set up or post to Company-sponsored blogs or microblogs, social networking pages, or other social media. Authorization is granted by _____
> _____ . Before you begin posting content, you must attend social media training.

Who Owns That Twitter Handle?

Often, it's perfectly clear that a social media page, website, or Twitter feed is corporate. For example, if a company's website has a blog or Facebook page, and a number of employees post work-related items on the company's behalf, any particular employee would have a hard time arguing that he or she "owned" the account.

However, the situation might look different if a particular account is closely identified with a particular employee, especially if that employee takes steps to mingle the personal and professional. Here are a couple of recent examples:

- Noah Kravitz started a Twitter account while he was employed at PhoneDog. The account was under his name (PhoneDog_Noah), he linked it to his personal email account, and he posted items both personal and professional. When he left the company, he changed his handle to NoahKravitz and kept tweeting on the account. PhoneDog sued to stop him, arguing that his followers were a type of customer list, and therefore that Kravitz had misappropriated the company's trade secret.

- Linda Eagle, the founder of EdComm, opened a LinkedIn account in 2008. She used the account to promote the company and her own accomplishments, as well as to stay in touch with social and professional contacts; an EdComm employee had her account password and helped her maintain it. She left the company following a buyout, and EdComm changed her LinkedIn password and continued to use the account. Eagle sued for misappropriation of her account.

If you are bringing on employees with existing social media accounts that you'd like them to use for business, or if your employees mingle personal with business posts on an account that you believe belongs to your company, you can clarify ownership of the account through a written agreement. As this area of law is just beginning to develop, you should talk to a lawyer if you're facing this issue.

Guidelines for Posting

Your policy should provide some basic guidance for employees who post on company-sponsored sites and pages. After all, you don't want an employee to announce a deal on the company blog that hasn't yet been finalized, disclose marketing secrets related to an unreleased product, or use copyrighted images from a hot movie trailer without permission. At the same time, you want employees to post content that's interesting, relevant, and reflects positively on your company.

The sample policy language below includes some common guidelines for employee posts.

Guidelines for Employees Who Post

1. **Be respectful.** When you post about the Company, its products and employees, customers, and competitors, use good judgment. Make sure your posts are professional and respectful. It's fine to disagree, as long as you do so in a civil way and you're not offensive.

2. **Add value.** We expect you to write about new developments and trends in your area of expertise. Don't just recycle news or posts; add your perspective and provide useful advice to enable consumers to better use our products and services.

3. **Post often.** We want readers to return and see what's new at our Company, and the best way you can help make that happen is to post at least weekly.

4. **Be part of the conversation.** When appropriate, link to other sites, articles, blogs, and media on the same topic. And of course, link to our Company site when appropriate.

---

5. **Accuracy counts.** Before you publish a blog post or a social media entry, review it for accuracy. When writing about Company business, check with the appropriate people in-house to make sure you've got the facts straight. If you later learn you've made a mistake, say so—and correct it.

6. **Avoid inappropriate topics.** We want you to generate interest, but there are many ways to do that without offending readers or placing the Company in the midst of a controversy. All company policies, including those that prohibit harassment, discrimination, and unprofessional conduct, apply with equal force to your online posts.

7. **Respect ownership of intellectual property.** Don't copy or use work by someone else (including text, photos, and video) without proper authorization and, if required, attribution. If you're referring to a copyrighted story, keep your quotes short; if you want to refer to another's work, it's best to link to it in its entirety.

8. **Keep the company's secrets.** Don't refer to or reveal the company's trade secrets and proprietary information. This includes stock offerings, financials, products in development, and other confidential information. If you aren't sure whether to reveal particular information in your post, speak to your manager.

9. **Maintain customer and employee privacy.** Do not mention customers by name or identifying details without authorization from your manager. If you want to discuss or mention coworkers in your posts, you must get their permission first.

10. **Ask—and think—before you post.** Remember, your posted content represents you and the Company to the public—and all of us want that representation to be positive. If you aren't certain that what you plan to post is appropriate and legal, check with your manager before you post.

Defamation in 140 Characters or Less

Some people find it hard to express themselves or say anything meaningful within the 140-character limit set by Twitter. Others, apparently, can say enough to spark a lawsuit (or at least the threat of one). Here are a few examples of alleged defamation by Tweet:

- In what may be the first Twitter lawsuit, Courtney Love was served with legal papers after reportedly using her Twitter account to call fashion designer Dawn Simorangkir a prostitute, drug addict, and "nasty lying hosebag thief." (And those are only seven of the words ...).

- Amanda Bonnen tweeted her friend to say, "Who said sleeping in a moldy apartment is bad for you? Horizon realty thinks it's okay." Horizon, which owned the apartment building where she lived, was not amused: It sued her for libel and asked for $50,000 in damages. The irony: Before the lawsuit, Bonnen's Twitter feed (and the allegedly libelous comments) were seen only by Horizon and her reported 20 followers; once the lawsuit was filed and the story picked up by the *Chicago Sun Times*, thousands more readers learned about Bonnen's "moldy apartment."

- Kim Kardashian got slapped with a lawsuit by Dr. Sanford Siegel, originator of "the cookie diet." According to published reports, Siegel's site linked to an article in which someone claimed that Kardashian was on the diet. Kardashian responded on Twitter, saying "Dr. Siegel's Cookie Diet is falsely promoting that I'm on this diet. NOT TRUE! I would never do this unhealthy diet. I do Quick Trim!" Siegel sued for libel over nine of those characters: the ones that spell "unhealthy."

Authorship and Disclaimers

In the recent past, the Internet allowed only one-way communication. A company developed a basic website that provided information and perhaps allowed customers to place orders, and that was it. No individual names were associated with the site: It represented the company as a whole.

With the advent of Web 2.0, however, the monologue has become a discussion. Social media allows many voices to speak and respond to each other—and readers want to know who those voices are. These new communication tools place a premium on point of view, perspective, and personality. That's why most companies that have a social media presence ask employees to identify themselves by name and title, as the policy language below does.

Identify Yourself

When you post any type of content to Company-sponsored social media, for example, our Facebook or Twitter pages, you must identify yourself by name and by your position at the Company. Anonymous posting or posting under pseudonyms or aliases is prohibited. The same rule applies if you are posting comments on behalf of the Company to one of our competitor's social media accounts, websites, or product pages.

> ⓘ **CAUTION**
>
> **Employees must reveal their employment relationship when posting comments about your company or its products.** The Federal Trade Commission, which interprets and enforces the laws prohibiting deceptive advertising, recently released regulatory guidelines on product endorsements, including those that appear in social media. The rules make clear that employees who discuss their company's products in online posts—for example, a comment to a blog or social networking page—must identify themselves as company employees, to avoid leading other readers to believe that they are just ordinary consumers who happen to LOVE what your company makes. For more on these rules, see Chapter 6.

Some companies also require employees to post a conspicuous disclaimer on their company blogs or comments to social media pages, stating that the posted content represents their own views, not necessarily the views of the company. From a legal perspective, it's not clear that a disclaimer like this carries much weight. If the employee is posting on company time and the company dime, chances are very good that the company will be vicariously liable for the employee's activities—particularly if the company's name appears on the masthead of the blog or page.

On the other hand, requiring employees to post a disclaimer has a couple of benefits. First of all, it reminds employees to take responsibility for what they post. Your company may well be liable for what employees post, but it won't be alone at the defense table: The employee could also be personally liable for posts that break the law or cause personal injury (such as defamation or harm to reputation). Second, it signals to customers (and your stockholders) that the company doesn't necessarily agree with every opinion an employee puts into the blogosphere, which may prove helpful if you need to distance yourself from a post for public relations reasons. Include the language below in your policy if you want employees to claim their opinions for themselves.

You Are Responsible for Your Posts

Remember, you are legally responsible for what you post online, whether on a personal site or a Company-sponsored site. You can be held personally liable for defaming others, revealing trade secrets, and copyright infringement, among other things. All Company policies apply to your online posts on company-sponsored sites.

All employees who post content to Company sites and pages must include the following disclaimer:

"The posts on this page express my own views and opinion, and do not necessarily reflect the views of [*company name*]."

Employer Sued for Employee's Blog Posts: The Patent Troll Tracker Affair

Rick Frenkel, a lawyer who worked as the director of intellectual property at Cisco Systems, maintained a blog under the name "Patent Troll Tracker," in which he wrote about patent trolls: a derogatory term for someone who sues for patent infringement but who does not make or sell any products using the patented technology. The blog's author was anonymous until Frenkel revealed his name and affiliation with Cisco, following the posting of a $15,000 "bounty" for his identification.

Once Frenkel's identity was known, he, Cisco, and two of its executives were sued over blog posts that allegedly disparaged attorneys who filed a patent suit against Cisco. Frenkel's blog was anonymous; it was not an official company blog nor did it appear on the company's website. Nonetheless, Cisco eventually took responsibility for the blog posts and Frenkel was dropped from the lawsuit, which settled.

Handling Comments

One of the features that make social media unique is the ability for readers to respond with comments. When your company has blogs, pages on networking sites such as Facebook, or a Twitter feed, third parties can join the conversation—and that conversation is memorialized under your company's name. This can be enormously helpful in building community, word of mouth, and loyalty among your company's customers. But it can also mean pages littered with spam, unfounded criticisms, and outright ranting.

If your company doesn't yet have a blog, you will be amazed by the amount of spam you receive as comments—and by the percentage of actual comments that are so inappropriate as to be unprintable. One way to handle this is to simply turn off the comments feature. This serves the purpose of keeping unwanted content off your site, as well as saving you the time and resources of screening comments. However, it also defeats one of the goals of participating in social media in the first place: creating an interactive relationship. And, for social networking sites like a Facebook fan page, turning off comments altogether is difficult and removing selected comments is nearly impossible (without soliciting Facebook's help). People come to these sites to communicate and participate.

Another way to handle comments is to moderate them, allowing all comments that are legitimate (that is, they aren't spam or an advertising link to another site) and not offensive. (Or, as Intel's Social Media Guidelines put it, post "the Good, the Bad, but not the Ugly.") What you don't want to do is pick and choose among comments, posting only the most flattering and sending complaints or criticisms to the virtual garbage bin. You absolutely should screen for appropriateness (in other words, do not allow offensive, biased, or foul-mouthed comments), but disallowing civil criticism will quickly gain your company a reputation for silencing the collective voice of the Internet: the deadliest sin in the world of Web 2.0.

Deleting Critical Comments Leads to Trouble

Above all else, social media participants seem to hate anything that smacks of censorship. A company that refuses to post—or, worse yet, takes down or threatens to take down—comments from readers with a bone to pick will soon find themselves on the wrong end of a TwitStorm.

That's what happened to food manufacturing giant Nestle, which was targeted by Greenpeace for using palm oil in its products. First, Nestle tried to quash a Greenpeace video (the video apparently likened eating a KitKat bar to eating an orangutan). A number of Greenpeace supporters then changed their Facebook photos to look like the company's logos, only with an anti-Nestle bent, then posted critical comments on Nestle's Facebook page. Nestle threatened to take down any comments that used such logos, responding that it had the right to control content on its site. The result? More angry posts, lost customers, a public relations nightmare, and an eventual agreement by Nestle to "ensure that its products have no deforestation footprint."

This doesn't mean you have to allow complaints and critiques to stand without a response, but you should instruct employees who post for your company to take those complaints to the appropriate person or department—and to resist the urge to "take on" the dissatisfied customer in the comments field. Having a long back-and-forth on a company-sponsored site about whether a product works as advertised or how dark its "dark red" upholstery really is won't successfully promote your company.

If you decide to allow moderated comments, use option 1, below. As you'll see, this option also tells employees how to handle complaints and criticism that comes in through the comments feature.

To disallow comments entirely, you can use option 2. Obviously, this option will work only for sites for which you can control the comments features, such as business blogs, some Facebook pages, and individual videos at You Tube. It may not be possible with other social media such as Twitter, for example.

Option 1: Moderated Comments

Handling Comments

We encourage reader responses and comments to our social media postings. However, not all reader commentary is fit to print. If you post entries that elicit reader responses or comments, you must follow these guidelines:

1. Do not allow the posting of spam, advertisements, or comments that merely link to another website (unless they are responsive to the original post).

2. Do not allow the posting of any comment that is obscene or offensive.

3. Do not allow the posting of any comment that reveals trade secrets or proprietary information. For example, if a competitor's employee reveals that company's confidential information in a comment, remove it immediately and report it to your manager.

4. Do not remove relevant anti-Company comments simply because they are negative. Do not engage in online arguments or "flame wars" through social media commenting. Talk to your manager about how—and through which medium—to respond appropriately.

5. If you receive a complaint about the company or its products in a comment, immediately notify [*department responsible for handling complaints, such as "the customer service team"*], so it can handle the situation directly.

Option 2: No Comments

> **Handling Comments**
>
> Because of the time and resources it would require to screen comments to our Company's blog(s), we do not post reader comments. Please turn off the "comments" feature of any Company blog to which you post content or for any other social media site at which you post (and for which comments can be removed).

Putting It All Together: A Sample Company-Sponsored Social Media Policy

Here's a sample social media policy for a training company that has its own blogs, Facebook fan page, and Twitter account. A handful of employees post content on the company's behalf. The company is trying to position itself as a thought leader, and so wants to allow comments and interaction with consumers.

Company-Sponsored Social Media Policy

Our Company's Social Media Presence

Social media tools, including Company-sponsored blogs and micro-blogs, social networking sites, video or picture sharing sites, wikis, and other means of communicating online, are an important part of our Company's face to the public. These social media offer opportunities to shape opinion about our products and our company, to communicate directly with customers and clients, to provide added value for our customers, and to be part of the online conversation about important developments in our field.

We want to use social media to demonstrate the need for corporate training using statistics, studies, and current news items. We want to demonstrate that we are up-to-date on developments in our field. We also want to engage consumers by showing them the tremendous variety in training methods and media, through online video, podcasts, and other demonstrations of our work.

Who May Post

Only authorized employees may set up or post to Company-sponsored blogs or microblogs, social networking pages, or other social media. Authorization is granted by the Director of Online Marketing. Before you begin posting content, you must attend social media training.

Guidelines for Employees Who Post

1. **Be respectful.** When you post about the Company, its products and employees, customers, and competitors, use good judgment. Make sure your posts are professional and respectful. It's fine to disagree, as long as you do so in a civil way and you're not offensive.

2. **Add value.** We expect you to write about new developments and trends in your area of expertise. Don't just recycle news or posts; add your perspective and provide useful advice to enable consumers to better use our products and services.

3. **Post often.** We want readers to return and see what's new at our Company, and the best way you can help make that happen is to post at least weekly.

4. **Be part of the conversation.** When appropriate, link to other sites, articles, blogs, and media on the same topic. And of course, link to our Company site when appropriate.

5. **Accuracy counts.** Before you publish a blog post or a social media entry, review it for accuracy. When writing about Company business, check with the appropriate people in-house to make sure you've got the facts straight. If you later learn you've made a mistake, say so—and correct it.

6. **Avoid inappropriate topics.** We want you to generate interest, but there are many ways to do that without offending readers or placing the Company in the midst of a controversy. All company policies, including those that prohibit harassment, discrimination, and unprofessional conduct, apply with equal force to your online posts.

7. **Respect ownership of intellectual property.** Don't copy or use work by someone else (including text, photos, and video) without proper authorization and, if required, attribution. If you're referring to a copyrighted story, keep your quotes short; if you want to refer to another's work, it's best to link to it in its entirety.

8. **Keep the company's secrets.** Don't refer to or reveal the company's trade secrets and proprietary information. This includes stock offerings, financials, products in development, and other confidential information. If you aren't sure whether to reveal particular information in your post, speak to your manager.

9. **Maintain customer and employee privacy.** Do not mention customers by name or identifying details without authorization from your manager. If you want to discuss or mention coworkers in your posts, you must get their permission first.

10. **Ask—and think—before you post.** Remember, your posted content represents you and the Company to the public—and all of us want that representation to be positive. If you aren't certain that what you plan to post is appropriate and legal, check with your manager before you post.

Identify Yourself

When you post any type of content to Company-sponsored social media, for example, our Facebook or Twitter pages, you must identify yourself by name and by your position at the Company. Anonymous posting or posting under pseudonyms or aliases is prohibited. The same rule applies if you are posting comments on behalf of the Company to one of our competitor's social media accounts, websites, or product pages.

You Are Responsible for Your Posts

Remember, you are legally responsible for what you post online, whether on a personal site or a company-sponsored site. You can be held personally liable for defaming others, revealing trade secrets, and copyright infringement, among other things. All Company policies apply to your online posts on company-sponsored sites.

All employees who post content to Company sites and pages must include the following disclaimer:

"The posts on this page express my own views and opinion, and do not necessarily reflect the views of TrainersEdge."

Handling Comments

We encourage reader responses and comments to our social media postings. However, not all reader commentary is fit to print. If you post entries that elicit reader responses or comments, you must follow these guidelines:

1. Do not allow the posting of spam, advertisements, or comments that merely link to another website (unless they are responsive to the original post).

2. Do not allow the posting of any comment that is obscene or offensive.

3. Do not allow the posting of any comment that reveals trade secrets or proprietary information. For example, if a competitor's employee reveals that company's confidential information in a comment, remove it immediately and report it to your manager.

4. Do not remove relevant anti-Company comments simply because they are negative. Do not engage in online arguments or "flame wars" through social media commenting. Talk to your manager about how—and through which medium—to respond appropriately.

5. If you receive a complaint about the company or its products in a comment, immediately notify the customer service department, so it can handle the situation directly.

Cell Phones

In This Chapter:

Policy Provisions for Cell Phones

☐ Security of Company-Issued Cell Phones

☐ Personal Cell Phones at Work

☐ Don't Use a Cell Phone While Driving

   ☐ Optional Policy Language for Hands-Free Equipment

☐ Using Your Cell Phone for Business

ell phones have changed the landscape of everyday life so much that it's hard to remember a time when they weren't everywhere. But that time wasn't so long ago. Cell phones didn't become a common consumer purchase until the 1990s or so, and even then few people used them as a primary means of communication. Today, however, the cell phone is a necessity of modern life. By 2011, there were more cell phones than people in the United States.

The First Call on a Portable Cell Phone

There was a lot going on in April 1973: France and the Netherlands recognized North Vietnam as a separate country; John Lennon and Yoko Ono formed their own country called Nutopia (its national anthem was silence, possibly preferable to the chart-topping single of the month, "Tie a Yellow Ribbon Round the Old Oak Tree," by Tony Orlando and Dawn); Richard Nixon announced the resignation of many of his top aides in the Watergate scandal; and Roberto Clemente's number was retired by the Pittsburgh Pirates. Oh, and Martin Cooper made the first public telephone call on a portable cell phone.

Of course, "portable" is in the eye of the beholder: The phone Cooper used weighed two and a half pounds and was ten inches long, and its battery died after 20 minutes. It was called "The Boot" because of its shape. At the time, Cooper worked for Motorola. He used his first phone call to contact a friend who worked at a rival company, AT&T's Bell Labs.

Unfortunately, the convenience of the cell phone can also be its curse—especially in the workplace. Cell phones can be distracting and disruptive at work, whether used in a shared workspace, during a business meeting, or while the owner should be helping customers or clients. They can even be dangerous—for example when used to transfer trade secrets, to eavesdrop in the company lunch room, or while driving. This chapter provides some policy language you can use to prevent common cell phone problems.

 RELATED TOPIC
This chapter covers only the "phone" feature of cell phones. Other chapters cover technologies that might be included with a cell phone, such as cameras (Chapter 10), instant messaging (Chapter 5), email (Chapter 3), and personal digital assistants (Chapter 9).

Company-Issued Phones

If your company is one of the many that issue cell phones to employees, you'll need policy language covering a few issues: company ownership of the phones, personal calls, and theft prevention.

Company Ownership of Phones

Your policy should start by telling employees that company-issued cell phones are company property, which employees must return upon request. This gives your company the ability to control the features on its cell phones (for example, to make sure that the employee's contact list can be erased remotely if the cell phone is stolen). It also establishes the company's right to inspect cell phones, if necessary, which in turn diminishes employees' expectations of privacy in company-issued cell phones.

Company-Issued Cell Phones

The Company may issue cell phones to employees whose jobs require them to make calls while away from work or require them to be accessible for work-related matters.

Cell phones issued by the Company are Company property. Employees must comply with Company requests to make their Company-issued cell phones available for any reason, including upgrades, replacement, or inspection. Employees who leave the Company for any reason must turn in their Company-issued cell phones.

Personal Use of Company Cell Phones

For a variety of reasons, the simplest policy is not to allow personal calls on company cell phones. Employees and managers won't have to review cell phone bills every month looking for numbers that aren't related to business. The company won't have to make judgment calls about how much personal use of a cell phone is too much. And calls made by customers, clients, and coworkers won't go straight to voicemail because an employee is too busy chatting with friends and family to pick up a work-related call.

Despite all the good reasons not to allow personal calls, however, an outright ban is impractical. Even the most conscientious employee may occasionally have to take a brief personal call. And allowing these calls—often, from a child, spouse, or partner who needs to check in—may help employees be more productive by alleviating pressing personal concerns. The policy below reflects those considerations.

Personal Use of Company-Issued Cell Phones

Company-issued cell phones are to be used only for business purposes. Although occasional, brief personal phone calls using a Company-issued phone are permitted, personal use that exceeds this standard will result in discipline, up to and including termination. Employees are expected to reimburse the Company for any costs or charges relating to personal use of their cell phones.

Security of Company-Issued Phones

Employees may have phones full of text messages and client contact information, and they need to know how to keep it private. Your policy should also explain what employees should do if their company-issued phones are stolen.

Security of Company-Issued Phones

Employees are responsible for the security of Company-issued cell phones and the information stored on them. Always keep your cell phone with you when traveling; never leave it unattended in your car or hotel room. If your Company-issued cell phone is lost or stolen, notify the IT department immediately. Never store confidential Company information on a cell phone.

When using a cell phone, remember that your conversations are not necessarily private. Those around you can hear your end of the conversation. To protect the confidentiality of Company information (and avoid annoying others), please make cell phone calls in a private place.

Cell phone transmissions may be intercepted. For this reason, employees should not conduct highly sensitive or confidential conversations by cell phone. If you have any questions about what types of conversations are appropriate for a cell phone and which are not, please ask your manager.

Personal Cell Phones at Work

Most of your employees probably have personal cell phones that they bring to work. Apparently the main thing employees do at work with their personal cell phones—based on surveys—is annoy each other. These workplace annoyances result from loud ring tones, inappropriate personal conversations, interruptions to meetings and presentations, and rudeness to coworkers or customers while talking on the phone.

Some companies respond to these concerns by simply banning personal cell phones at work. For most employers, however, an outright ban is overkill. Allowing personal cell phones gives employees a chance to touch base with family members and friends while on breaks or at lunch, or to receive emergency messages during the day, all without using company phones. You can probably achieve the results you want—fewer interruptions and less time wasted—while allowing employees to have their cell phones at work by simply prohibiting employees from using cell phones (or allowing them to ring) at certain times, in particular locations, or for excessive amounts of time.

The policy language below contains basic cell phone etiquette for the workplace that most companies will want to adopt. Note that this policy addresses only personal use of personal phones; for policy language on employees using their personal phones and other devices for work, see Chapter 9.

Personal Cell Phones at Work

Although our Company allows employees to bring their personal cell phones to work, we expect employees to keep personal conversations to a minimum. While occasional, brief personal phone calls are acceptable, frequent or lengthy personal calls can affect productivity and disturb others. For this reason, we generally expect employees to make and receive personal phone calls during breaks only.

Employees must turn off the ringers on their cell phones while away from their cell phones. If you share workspace with others, you must turn off the ringer on your phone while at work.

Employees must turn off their cell phones or leave their phones elsewhere while in meetings, presentations, or trainings. Employees must also turn off their cell phones or leave their phones elsewhere while meeting with clients or serving customers.

It is inappropriate to interrupt a face-to-face conversation with a coworker in order to take a personal phone call.

Remember, others can hear your cell phone conversations. Try to talk quietly, and save intimate discussions for another time.

Employees who violate this policy will be subject to discipline, up to and including termination.

Annoying Ringtones: One of the Top Workplace Peeves

Since employees started bringing their cell phones to work, they've been annoying their coworkers with loud ringtones. According to a recent study by Randstad USA, employees find loud noises, including cell phone ring tones, to be one of the seven biggest pet peeves. Gossip, poor time management by coworkers, messiness in communal spaces (the Company kitchen or break room, for instance), potent scents, misuse of email, and overuse of personal communication devices—such as smart phones and cell phones—during meetings round out the list.

Safety

Studies show that drivers who are distracted cause more accidents, and that cell phones and other forms of wireless technology are increasingly to blame for our lack of attention to the road. Although recent surveys show that fewer people use cell phones when driving than in the past, well over half of all drivers admit they still do it, at least occasionally.

One Year, 100 Cars, 241 Drivers, and 82 Crashes

To get a better idea of why people get into car accidents, the National Highway Transportation Safety Association and the Virginia Tech Transportation Institute created an experiment: They put video and sensor equipment in 100 cars and tracked driver behavior for a year. And an eventful year it was, with more than two million miles driven, 82 crashes, 761 near-crashes, and more than 8,000 "critical incidents" (situations when the driver either got too close to another car,

One Year, 100 Cars, 241 Drivers, and 82 Crashes (continued)

pedestrian, cyclist, animal, or object, or had to engage in crash avoidance behavior—swerving, braking, and so on—to stay out of trouble).

The study revealed that almost 80% of crashes involved some form of driver distraction or drowsiness, and the number one source of driver distraction was using a cell phone. A few more interesting facts:

- **Dialing is dangerous but ...** Although dialing a cell phone is significantly more dangerous than simply talking or listening on the phone, the number of accidents and near-accidents attributable to each activity was about the same because drivers spend so much more time talking and listening on the phone than dialing it.

- **Don't let a bug in the car—or try to swat it once it's there.** Reaching for a moving object makes a driver nine times more likely to get in an accident. Reading, applying makeup, and dialing a cell phone each increase the risk of an accident by a factor of three, but having an insect in the car increased the risk by a factor of seven.

- **Experience counts.** Drivers with more years of experience had far fewer crashes and near-crashes than relatively inexperienced drivers.

- **Better drivers just seem nicer.** Better drivers—those with fewer crashes and near-crashes—scored higher on tests that measured extroversion, openness to experience, agreeableness, and conscientiousness.

- **Don't hire this guy.** A relatively small number of drivers caused most of the problems: 27 of the drivers in the test were responsible for almost 75% of the crashes and near-crashes; one of them had 15 incidents in one year.

To address these concerns, a growing number of states have passed laws that limit the use of cell phones while driving. These laws take several forms: Some require drivers to use a hands-free device if they want to talk on the phone, some prohibit younger or less experienced drivers from using any type of cell phone, and some allow officers to cite drivers for using a hand-held cell phone if the driver is pulled over for another offense.

> **TIP**
>
> **Keep up on the laws of your state.** For detailed information on state driving safety laws, check out the website of the Governors Highway Safety Association at www.statehighwaysafety.org. Select "State Laws & Funding" to see state law charts on a number of topics, including use of cell phones. The site, which is updated frequently, also has a number of other resources, including research and reports on various driver safety issues. Note that some local governments have also enacted cell phone restrictions, so check with your town, city, or county as well.

If your company does business in a state that limits the use of cell phones while driving, of course you'll want to require employees to follow the law. However, even companies in states that haven't legislated in this area need a cell phone policy. Simply put, using a cell phone while driving is dangerous. And, if an employee causes an accident while doing business on a cell phone, your company could be held liable for the damages.

Cell Phones + Driving Employees = Company Liability

There have been plenty of big settlements in lawsuits against companies whose employees injured or killed someone while talking on a cell phone. Why are the companies sued? Because they typically have much deeper pockets than the employee who actually caused the accident. Consider these examples:

- A stockbroker from Smith Barney was making a cold call to a potential client while driving when he struck and killed a motorcyclist. Although the broker was using his own cell phone and driving to a nonbusiness event, the plaintiff argued that Smith Barney should be found liable because it encouraged employees to use their cell phones for cold calling without training them on safety issues. Smith Barney eventually settled the case for $500,000.

- A lawyer was making a business call on her cell phone while driving home from work. She hit something, which she thought was a deer, and kept driving; sadly, she actually hit—and killed—a teenager. The attorney served a year in jail for hit-and-run driving and was ordered to pay the victim's family more than $2 million; her law firm settled its part of the case for an undisclosed amount.

- An employee of International Paper was using her company cell phone when she rear-ended another driver on the freeway, causing injuries that eventually required the other driver to have her arm amputated. The company paid $5.2 million to settle the case.

- An Illinois state trooper crashed head-on into another vehicle, killing two sisters. He pleaded guilty to reckless homicide and reckless driving and was sentenced to 30 months of probation; evidence was presented that he was driving 126 miles per hour, sending email on the car's computer, and using his cell phone when the crash took place. The girls' family sued him and his employer, the State of Illinois, in 2010 for $46 million in damages.

It really doesn't matter whether your company issues cell phones to employees or not: If your company's employees do business by phone, your company needs a cell phone policy. Not only will this help protect the safety of company employees and those they might encounter on the road, but it will also help your company avoid liability for accidents.

Don't Use a Cell Phone While Driving

We know that our employees may use their cell phones for work-related matters, whether these devices belong to the employee or are issued by the Company.

Employees are prohibited from using cell phones for work-related matters while driving. We are concerned for your safety and for the safety of other drivers and pedestrians, and using a cell phone while driving can lead to accidents.

If you must make a work-related call while driving, you must wait until you can pull over safely and stop the car before placing your call. If you receive a work-related call while driving, you must ask the caller to wait while you pull over safely and stop the car. If you are unable to pull over safely, you must tell the caller that you will have to call back when it is safe to do so.

If your company wants to allow employees to use a hands-free device to talk on the phone while driving, you can add the language below to the end of the policy. If your company issues cell phones to employees for work-related calls, it should also issue them hands-free equipment to allow them to use the phones in accordance with this part of the policy. Keep in mind, however, that some studies have shown that the use of hands-free equipment does not significantly eliminate the risk of accidents from talking on a cell phone.

Currently, no state prohibits adult, experienced drivers from using hands-free devices while driving, except for certain professions (such as school bus drivers). Before you adopt the policy language below, check on the laws of your state and local government to make sure that hands-free devices are still allowed.

> **Hands-Free Equipment**
>
> Employees may use hands-free equipment to make or answer calls while driving without violating this policy. However, safety must always be your first priority. We expect you to keep these calls brief. If, because of weather, traffic conditions, or any other reason, you are unable to concentrate fully on the road, you must either end the conversation or pull over and safely park your vehicle before resuming your call.

Wage and Hour Concerns

As portable technology improves, it's becoming easier for employees to work anywhere, at almost any time. The benefits of this trend are obvious: higher productivity, opportunities for telecommuting, improved work-life balance for employees, even reducing greenhouse gases as fewer employees have to commute each day.

There's a significant legal downside to consider, however. When nonexempt employees—those who are entitled to earn overtime—work away from their usual worksite, those hours might not get recorded, and the employee may not receive overtime pay, in violation of wage and hour laws.

The Fair Labor Standards Act (FLSA) is the federal law that governs wages and hours. Among other things, the FLSA requires employers to pay nonexempt employees overtime if they work more than 40 hours in a week; some state laws have daily overtime standards. Employees must be paid for every hour the employer "suffers or permits" them to work. This rule has been interpreted fairly strictly against employers: If employees are working overtime hours, and your company knows or should know about it, the employees are entitled to overtime pay.

Cell phones create a problem because employees can use them anywhere at any time. Employees who make a few work-related calls on the weekend or after hours might be entitled to overtime. This is true whether they use their own phones or a phone issued by the company. And, it will be tough for the company to find out about these extra hours until it's too late: Often, a company only discovers that an employee thinks he or she should have earned overtime when it is served with a lawsuit or complaint from the federal or state labor department. The best way to avoid these problems is to adopt a policy prohibiting employees from making unauthorized calls on their own time.

Using Your Cell Phone for Business

Our Company's overtime rules apply to any type of work done after hours, including using a Company-issued cell phone to make business calls. All overtime work—including such work-related calls—must be approved in writing, in advance. Working overtime without permission violates Company policy and may result in disciplinary action.

CAUTION

If they work, you must pay. Even if your company requires employees to get approval before working overtime, it should pay for the overtime hours they work—including hours that aren't authorized. Discipline employees who work unapproved overtime, but pay them for those hours. This is a much safer approach than having to argue later, to a labor commissioner or judge, that your company didn't "suffer or permit" the work.

> ⊘ **CAUTION**
>
> **Don't forget the acknowledgment form.** If your company adopts the cell phone policy covered in this chapter, make sure you require employees to sign an acknowledgment form. You'll find a sample acknowledgment form and instructions online at this book's companion page on Nolo's website; see the appendix for more information.

Putting It All Together: Sample Cell Phone Policy

Here's a sample cell phone policy adopted by a company that sells and repairs office equipment. The company has issued cell phones to its sales and service staff, who make numerous work-related calls every day and are often away from the office. Because employees spend much of their day driving to and from client businesses, the company is also very concerned about driving safety—so much so that it decides not to allow cell phone use while driving, even with hands-free devices.

Cell Phone Policy

Company-Issued Cell Phones

The Company may issue cell phones to employees whose jobs require them to make calls while away from work or require them to be accessible for work-related matters.

Cell phones issued by the Company are Company property. Employees must comply with Company requests to make their Company-issued cell phones available for any reason, including upgrades, replacement, or inspection. Employees who leave the Company for any reason must turn in their Company-issued cell phones.

Personal Use of Company-Issued Cell Phones

Company-issued cell phones are to be used only for business purposes. Although occasional, brief personal phone calls using a Company-issued phone are permitted, personal use that exceeds this standard will result in discipline, up to and including termination. Employees are expected to reimburse the Company for any costs or charges relating to personal use of their cell phones.

Security of Company-Issued Phones

Employees are responsible for the security of Company-issued cell phones and the information stored on them. Always keep your cell phone with you when traveling; never leave it unattended in your car or hotel room. If your Company-issued cell phone is lost or stolen, notify the IT department immediately. Never store confidential Company information on a cell phone.

When using a cell phone, remember that your conversations are not necessarily private. Those around you can hear your end of the conversation. To protect the confidentiality of Company information (and avoid annoying others), please make cell phone calls in a private place.

Cell phone transmissions may be intercepted. For this reason, employees should not conduct highly sensitive or confidential conversations by cell phone. If you have any questions about what types of conversations are appropriate for a cell phone and which are not, please ask your manager.

Personal Cell Phones at Work

Although our Company allows employees to bring their personal cell phones to work, we expect employees to keep personal conversations to a minimum. While occasional, brief personal phone calls are acceptable, frequent or lengthy personal calls can affect productivity and disturb others. For this reason, we generally expect employees to make and receive personal phone calls during breaks only.

Employees must turn off the ringers on their cell phones while away from their cell phones. If you share workspace with others, you must turn off the ringer on your phone while at work.

Employees must turn off their cell phones or leave their phones elsewhere while in meetings, presentations, or trainings. Employees must also turn off their cell phones or leave their phones elsewhere while meeting with clients or serving customers.

It is inappropriate to interrupt a face-to-face conversation with a coworker in order to take a personal phone call.

Remember, others can hear your cell phone conversations. Try to talk quietly, and save intimate discussions for another time.

Employees who violate this policy will be subject to discipline, up to and including termination.

Don't Use a Cell Phone While Driving

We know that our employees may use their cell phones for work-related matters, whether these devices belong to the employee or are issued by the Company.

Employees are prohibited from using cell phones for work-related matters while driving. We are concerned for your safety and for the safety of other drivers and pedestrians, and using a cell phone while driving can lead to accidents.

If you must make a work-related call while driving, you must wait until you can pull over safely and stop the car before placing your call. If you receive a work-related call while driving, you must ask the caller to wait while you pull over safely and stop the car. If you are unable to pull over safely, you must tell the caller that you will have to call back when it is safe to do so.

Using Your Cell Phone for Business

Our Company's overtime rules apply to any type of work done after hours, including using a Company-issued cell phone to make business calls. All overtime work—including such work-related calls—must be approved in writing, in advance. Working overtime without permission violates Company policy and may result in disciplinary action.

Portable Computing Devices: Smart Phones, Laptops, Tablets, and Beyond

In This Chapter:

Policy Provisions for Portable Computing Devices

Rules for Company-Issued Devices

☐ Personal Use of Portable Computing Devices

☐ Use of Portable Computing Devices Is Not Private

☐ Content Rules for Portable Computing Devices

☐ Security of Portable Computing Devices

☐ No Texting While Driving

☐ Overtime and Portable Computing Devices

Rules for BYOD

☐ Option 1: Don't Use Personal Mobile Devices for Work

☐ Option 2: Using Personal Mobile Devices for Work

    ☐ How Employees Will Use BYOD

    ☐ Your Personal Information

    ☐ Security of Personal Mobile Devices

    ☐ Reimbursing Employees

    ☐ No Texting While Driving

    ☐ Overtime and Personal Mobile Devices

As processing power grows and microchip size shrinks, the tech world is witnessing a convergence of portable computing devices. Handheld personal digital assistants (PDAs) like the BlackBerry are packed with more software and memory, while laptop computers are shrinking in size. And tablets, whether for use primarily as e-book readers or mobile computers, are increasingly popular.

There is no single name for all of these portable computing devices, but whether you call them smartphones, laptops, handhelds, or PDAs, they have something in common: Employees use them to do their jobs remotely, at home, and on the road.

Like the other technologies discussed in this book, however, portable computing devices bring increased risk with their increased efficiency. The most significant of these risks is from the theft or loss of company information. The very portability of these devices makes them a target for thieves—and all too easy to leave behind in a cab, restaurant, hotel room, or bar (iPhone prototype, anyone?). These devices may also expose the company's network to risks (if they can link into the company servers) and provide a backdoor for opportunistic hackers and viruses.

Because these devices are intended to allow employees to work away from the office, they can also create potentially huge liability for overtime work that the company doesn't know about or pay for. Finally, like cell phones, these devices can lead to safety problems and legal exposure for the company if employees use them while driving.

All of these risks are present whether employees use phones and other devices provided by your company or use their own personal devices for work. But the risks are multiplied in the latter scenario, often referred to as BYOD (for "bring your own device"). If employees use their own smart phones or other mobile devices for business and pleasure, your company will have to figure out what devices and uses it will allow, how it can maintain security and ownership of its information, and how to handle employee expenses, among other things.

Although many of the same considerations apply to Company-issued and personal devices, your company has a lot more control over devices it provides—and the privacy and security concerns are less complicated. This chapter starts with policy provisions for company-provided devices, then covers BYOD.

Rules for Company-Issued Devices

If your company issues any portable devices to employees, it should adopt policy language covering those devices. This is true whether or not your company also allows BYOD.

User Rules for Company-Issued Devices

Like other types of company-issued technology, portable computing devices can easily be put to personal use. Employees may use their company smartphones to call and text friends and family, their company laptops to send personal email and chat on the Internet, or their electronic readers to review their Great American Novel. Your company should make clear that its policies on appropriate use apply with equal force to the portable computing devices it issues. You should also cover personal use of company equipment. And, your policy must make clear that employees have no right to privacy in what they write or store on company-issued portable devices.

Personal Use

There's no way around it: Employees are likely to use portable computing devices for personal reasons. That's why your company needs a policy on personal use of these devices. Like the policies in earlier chapters for email and the Internet, the policy language below allows limited personal use, but also warns employees that excessive use will led to discipline. It also requires employees to reimburse your company for more than occasional personal use.

Personal Use of Company-Issued Portable Computing Devices

The Company may provide you with a portable computing device (such as a laptop computer, tablet, smartphone, personal digital assistant, or [*if your company uses an industry-specific device, add it here*]). The Company may also permit you to access its network using a portable computing device to perform your job.

The Company's portable computing devices and network are intended for business use. You may use such computing devices for occasional personal purposes, but you may do so during nonwork hours only. You must also ensure that your personal use of the company's portable computing devices does not interfere in any way with your job duties or performance. Any employee who abuses this privilege may be subject to discipline, up to and including termination.

If an employee's use of a Company-issued portable computing device results in fees or costs beyond what the Company would otherwise have to pay for the service, the employee will be required to reimburse the Company.

Privacy

Your policy must also warn employees that they have no privacy in the information stored on Company-issued portable computing devices. (See Chapters 1 and 3 for information about employee privacy and Company-issued equipment.)

Use of Portable Computing Devices Is Not Private

The Company has the ability to access and review all information stored on the Company's portable computing devices and network. The Company reserves the right to perform such an inspection at any time, for any reason. You should not expect that any files, records, or other data stored on the Company's equipment and network will be private, even if you attempt to protect its privacy (for example, by using a password or designating it as "personal").

Appropriate Content

You need not repeat all of the content rules for the various capabilities of portable computing devices (email, instant messaging, and Internet access, for example). Instead, you can refer back to those policies here, with a reminder that they apply to Company-issued portable computing devices as well.

Content Rules for Portable Computing Devices

All of our policies and rules of conduct apply to employee use of Company-issued portable computing devices. All communications (email, instant messaging, and Internet access) on Company-issued portable computing devices are subject to the Company's policies on appropriate use. This means, for example, that employees may not send harassing messages, access pornographic or gambling websites, or violate any of the Company's other rules on appropriate communications content.

Security of Company-Issued Devices

Because of their small size and portability, laptops, PDAs, and smartphones are easily lost or stolen. And, because they are often intended to allow employees to access the company's network remotely, these devices present virus and hacking threats, whether they remain in the employee's possession or fall into the wrong hands.

Employees need to know how to protect their portable devices and the data on them. Your policy should cover security issues such as encryption, theft prevention, and antivirus technology.

What Really Happens When You Lose Your Smartphone?

According to industry data, people lose their phones about once a year. Of course, some people find their phones again—and some get their phones back from the apparently well-meaning folks who find them.

But a recent study shows that those Good Samaritans who return lost phones to their owners are not so good after all. In 2012, Symantec deliberately "lost" 50 Android phones in Los Angeles, San Francisco, Washington, New York City, and Ottawa. The phones were loaded with fake data and stored passwords, and left unlocked. Then, Symantec tracked what happened to them.

The good news: About half of the phone-finders made at least some effort to return the phone. But not after digging through it like gold miners. Here's what else the study showed:

- 95% of the finders tried to access personal or sensitive information.
- 72% looked through stored photos, and 60% tried to get on Facebook and other social media sites.
- 57% accessed the fake list of passwords for the phone's services planted by Symantec.
- More than 40% tried to access banking and corporate email accounts, and more than half tried to access a fake list of "employee salaries."

CAUTION

Don't forget your reporting obligations. According to the National Conference of State Legislatures, 46 states and the District of Columbia have enacted notification statutes, which require companies to tell consumers if their personal information has been stolen or otherwise compromised. To find out what your state requires, go to the Conference's website, www.ncsl.org. Under the "Issues & Research" tab, select "Telecommunications/IT," then "Privacy & Security."

Use the policy below to tell employees how to secure the information on their company-issued portable computing devices.

Security of Company-Issued Portable Computing Devices

Although portable computing equipment (such as laptops, tablets, personal digital assistants, or smartphones) can greatly improve our communications and efficiency, they can also pose a risk to the security of the Company's proprietary information. If these devices are lost, stolen, or hacked into, an outsider could have access to Company data or the Company's network.

To prevent theft and loss of data, employees who receive Company-issued portable computing equipment must follow these guidelines:

Employees should not download confidential Company information to a portable computing device unless it is absolutely necessary. If confidential Company information is stored on a portable computing device, you must delete that information securely as soon as you are finished using it. If you are not certain whether particular data qualifies as confidential Company information, ask your supervisor for assistance.

All data and files kept on a portable computing device must be encrypted, using Company-approved encryption software.

All Company-issued portable computing devices will require power-on passwords, which must be changed every two months. You must always log or sign off before leaving a portable computing device unattended.

If your Company-issued portable computing device is equipped with antivirus software, you must download or install updates to this software when instructed by the Company.

You may not download, install, or use any software programs on a Company-issued portable computing device unless that program has been approved by the IT department.

Use the same malware precautions when using a portable computing device as are required for Company computers. Do not open attachments to email or instant messages if you do not know the sender or otherwise aren't sure that the attachment is legitimate. Do not open, read, or download any file from the Internet without scanning it for viruses.

Employees are responsible for the security of portable computing devices issued to them. Keep portable computing devices in your possession whenever possible. If you must leave a portable computing device unattended, you must store it out of sight in a secure location, such as a hotel safe or locked filing cabinet at home. Never leave a portable computing device in a vehicle.

Employees must immediately notify the Company's IT department if their portable computing device is lost or stolen, so the Company may remotely delete all data stored on the device.

International Employers: Don't Let Trade Secrets Slip Out at the Border

The 9th Circuit Court of Appeals recently ruled that U.S. Customs and Border Patrol agents can search the contents of a traveler's laptop even if they don't have any particular reason to suspect wrongdoing. In *U.S. v. Arnold*, No. 06-50581 (April 21, 2008), the Court found no reason to exclude evidence of child pornography that Border Patrol agents found on Michael Arnold's laptop when he arrived at Los Angeles International Airport after a trip to the Philippines. Although the Fourth Amendment of the U.S. Constitution requires reasonable suspicion to search, border searches are presumed reasonable because of the government's strong interest in preventing unwanted people and items entering the country.

Let's hope that your company's employees never find themselves in exactly this situation. Even so, if your employees take laptops, PDAs, or handheld digital devices on a foreign business trip, they risk losing those devices—and the information on them—to Border Patrol agents, who sometimes confiscate such items. Your company's proprietary information and personal data about employees or customers, may be seized.

How often are devices searched at the border? According to documents the American Civil Liberties Union received after making a Freedom of Information Act (FOIA) request, more than 6,500 devices were searched between October 2008 and June 2010. Cell phones were most likely to be searched, followed by laptops and digital cameras. And, in 280 cases, the border agents transferred data from the devices to other federal government agencies.

These numbers are relatively small, given the large number of personal devices that travel internationally every day. Nonetheless, experts advise companies to limit—and protect—the proprietary and personal data employees keep on the laptops and smartphones when crossing international borders.

Lessons From the Real World

Fall into the (liability) Gap: Stolen laptops compromise job applicant data.

Joel Ruiz applied for a job at one of Gap's clothing stores in 2006. As part of the application process, Ruiz provided personal information, including his Social Security number. In 2007, Gap notified Ruiz and 800,000 other applicants that two of its laptops, which contained their application data in unencrypted form, had been stolen. Gap offered each applicant a year of free credit monitoring and fraud assistance, along with some identity theft insurance.

Ruiz filed a class action lawsuit against Gap, claiming that the company acted negligently, violated his privacy, and committed an unfair business practice, among other things. Gap argued that Ruiz's claims should be thrown out. There was no proof that Ruiz's information had been accessed or used in any way, so he couldn't show that he had suffered actual harm—an essential element of a lawsuit.

Although the district court found that Ruiz had alleged enough harm, including an increased risk of identity theft, to continue with his suit, Ruiz eventually lost the case.

Ruiz v. Gap, Inc., 540 F.Supp.2d 1121 (N.D. Cal. 2008).

Driving Safety

Like cell phones, the use of PDAs and smartphones while driving can be very dangerous. In fact, texting while driving is more dangerous than talking on the phone, according to a study by the University of Utah: Those talking on a cell phone are four times more likely to get into an accident than people driving without distractions, while texting increases the likelihood of an accident by six times. The same study also shows that texting slows driver reaction times.

No DWT

One of the hottest issues in statehouses across the country these days is DWT: driving while texting. In just the last couple of years, more than half of the states have banned it outright for all drivers, and more ban texting for younger drivers only.

In some states, high-profile accidents may have helped push the legislation along. In Washington, for example, a driver was using his BlackBerry and failed to see that the traffic ahead of him on Interstate 5 had stopped; he crashed into a minivan, setting off a pileup that also involved four other cars and a bus. Several months later, the Washington legislature outlawed texting by drivers.

In New Jersey, the state legislature began considering its anti-texting law within a month after Governor Jon Corzine was badly injured in a car crash. Corzine, who was in the passenger seat, wasn't wearing his seat belt. What's more, his driver—who was doing 91 mph in a 65 zone—was investigated by state troopers who wanted to know whether he was texting (with his alleged girlfriend's husband) at the time of the accident.

You can find out what your state is up to at the website of the National Conference on State Legislatures, www.ncsl.org; select "Traffic Safety" in the "Transportation" issue area. Is legislation really necessary to prevent something so obviously dangerous? Unfortunately, yes: 85% of respondents to one survey said they would not DWT if it were illegal.

Despite the somewhat obvious fact that texting while driving is dangerous, however, more than half of all drivers admit to doing it. In response, many states have enacted bans on texting while driving. And companies are adopting policies prohibiting employees from doing so, too. Just like using a cell phone, texting while driving can lead to accidents—and to liability for your company.

No Texting While Driving

Employees are prohibited from using any Company-issued portable computing device for while driving. We are concerned for your safety and for the safety of other drivers and pedestrians, and texting, checking messages, going online, or otherwise using a portable computing device while driving can lead to accidents.

If you must send or read a message while driving, you must wait until you can pull over safely and stop the car before doing so.

Lessons From the Real World

If you don't know where you're going, pull over.

An employee of Berry Electric Contracting Company got lost while driving a company van in Arlington Heights, a Chicago suburb. He was trying to use the navigation device on his BlackBerry when he ran a red light and hit another car.

The driver of the other car, a 71-year-old woman, had to undergo five surgeries as a result of the crash. She lost some range of motion in her neck, has metal holding her pelvis together, and has permanent vision problems as a result of the crash. She sued the company. Right before trial, the case settled for $4.1 million, which was paid by Berry Electric's insurance carrier.

Abdon M. Pallasch, "$4 Mil. Award in BlackBerry Car Accident," *The Chicago Sun Times*, December 9, 2006.

Wage and Hour Concerns

Personal computing devices make it possible for employees to work offsite, 24 x 7 x 365. This ability to work overtime can open your company up to significant legal exposure for wage and hour claims.

When nonexempt employees—those who are entitled to earn overtime—work away from their usual worksite, those hours might not get recorded, and the employee may not receive overtime pay, in violation of wage and hour laws. Employees who check their email after hours or work on documents from home might be entitled to overtime. And, the company might not know about these extra hours until it hears from a lawyer. (For more detailed information on overtime liability, see Chapter 7.)

Time Off? Not Really

In 2012, Harris Interactive conducted a survey of employee work habits while on vacation. The results really put the lie to the notion of "time off": More than one-third of managers expected employees to check in with the office while on vacation. This figure means some employees will be in for an unpleasant beach surprise, as only 13% of employees expected to be asked to work while on vacation. Almost one-third of the employees surveyed expected to check work email while out, almost one-quarter expected to receive work-related phone calls, and almost one-fifth expected to get work-related texts.

The best way to control your company's liability is to adopt a policy requiring employees to get written authorization before using handheld computers or other portable technology outside of their usual hours.

Overtime and Portable Computing Devices

Our Company's overtime rules apply to any type of work done after hours, including using a Company-issued portable computing device (laptop, PDA, or smartphone, etc.) for work. All overtime work—including work done on a personal computing device—must be approved in writing, in advance. Working overtime without permission violates Company policy and may result in disciplinary action.

Personal Devices and BYOD

One of the hottest issues in workplace technology these days is BYOD: allowing employees to use their own mobile devices for both business and pleasure. Only a few years ago, BYOD was almost nonexistent. Companies were advised to ban employees from using their own devices for work. Companies issued work phones or corporate BlackBerrys to employees who needed them, and called it a day.

But employees love their personal devices, especially their iPhones. Companies reported increased demands by employees to use the devices they like and feel comfortable with for work purposes, rather than having to double up on their devices and abandon their favorite apps and platforms.

Makes sense, right? But the security, privacy, and management concerns associated with BYOD are complex. Industry experts disagree about how best to handle everything from protecting corporate data to reimbursing employee expenses. A lot of the legal issues and practical effects associated with BYOD are still emerging, as are the mobile device management (MDM) and mobile application management (MAM) software solutions that allow companies to protect their data. This section provides some basic policy language for BYOD. Before you decide on a corporate BYOD strategy and policy, however, you should consult with a lawyer to make sure you have the most up-to-date information and expertise in this rapidly changing area.

Just the Facts MAM

Most companies that conscientiously roll out a BYOD program choose a software solution (or more than one) to help maintain the security of company information. These solutions are evolving rapidly as the growth of BYOD has made the gaps in existing offerings painfully obvious. Currently, software options for controlling mobile devices—or the information on those devices—include:

- Mobile device management (MDM). Familiar to companies that have issued corporate BlackBerrys to employees, MDM software essentially gives the company control over the employee's entire phone or tablet. It's the most secure solution, and also the most likely to meet with employee resistance, as it gives the company access to and control over the employee's personal information.
- Mobile application management (MAM). Companies can use MAM software to control only the corporate apps and content loaded on the employee device. This means, among other things, that an employee won't have to enter a strong password just to make a personal phone call; instead, a password can be required only to access corporate apps and data. It also means that the company can wipe only its corporate information if the phone is lost.
- Mobile information management (MIM). Anyone who has used Dropbox is familiar with MIM, cloud-based systems that sync files among devices. This is a convenient and familiar option, but security remains a major concern (as anyone who has used Dropbox—or decided not to—probably also knows).

If your company chooses to go BYOD, one of your first steps should be creating a cross-departmental team, including IT, legal, and HR professionals, to choose the technical controls that will best meet your company's needs for security and flexibility.

To BYOD or Not to BYOD

Despite the growing popularity of BYOD, plenty of companies have decided not to offer it to employees. As explained below, BYOD comes with inherent security risks, which a company can't fully mitigate without employee cooperation. The privacy concerns that arise from BYOD are also significant, as employees' personal files and data reside on the same device as the company's files and data. This puts personal information at risk of being erased in a remote wipe, viewed in a corporate investigation or audit, and so on.

Given these problems, a number of companies have chosen not to allow BYOD, at least for now. This might make sense for companies in industries that don't require remote communication and networking, especially if they provide Company-issued devices to any employees whose jobs require them. Surveys show that, although many companies perceive that BYOD is very important to employees, they also worry about the inherent security risks—and for significant minority of companies, the risk outweighs the convenience and perceived morale boost of allowing BYOD.

Whether you have considered the issues and decided against BYOD or you simply haven't addressed the issue yet, you should adopt policy language prohibiting BYOD. Because personal computing devices are so common and so popular, employees are likely to use them for work whether or not company policy explicitly provides for it. The best strategy, if you don't want BYOD at your workplace, is to tell employees that it's prohibited.

Don't Use Personal Mobile Devices for Work

We understand that employees may occasionally wish to use their own mobile devices—such as smartphones or tablets—for work. However, storing Company information on a personal mobile device or using such a device to access the Company's network creates unacceptable security risks. Therefore, employees are prohibited from using their own mobile devices for business purposes or from storing Company information on a personal mobile device. If you feel that you need a mobile device to do your job, please talk to your manager to find out whether you are eligible for a Company-issued device.

Employee BYOD Practices: It's Not a Pretty Picture

Whether or not your company has a BYOD policy, employees are probably using their personal mobile devices for work. That is perhaps the least troubling finding of a 2012 Harris Interactive poll commissioned by ESET. Although two-thirds of the poll's respondents said their company did not have a BYOD policy, 81% used personal devices for work anyway. And the ways in which employees used their devices and accessed work-related information were unsafe at any speed:

- Almost half of the respondents who use a device for work had let someone else use it.
- More than a third had not activated the auto-lock feature of the device they use for work.
- About a third said the company data and files on their device were not encrypted.

These statistics are even more troubling when you consider how often people lose their personal devices, not to mention the possibility of hacking or corruption: One quarter of the respondents to the poll said they had been subjected to hacking or a malware attack on their personal device.

Which Devices Are Right for Your Company?

If you decide to adapt some form of BYOD policy, you'll need to tell employees which devices and platforms your company will allow. A consultation with the IT department—and perhaps an employee survey to find out which devices employees want to use—can help you answer this question. The sample policy language below addresses the most common BYOD devices. It also prohibits employees from using devices that have been altered to give users root access to the operating system, which leaves the device vulnerable to hacking and other security problems.

Using Personal Mobile Devices for Work

The Company allows employees to use their personal smartphones, tablets, and other mobile devices for work, in the circumstances set forth below. To protect the company's data and resources, only certain devices and uses are allowed.

Acceptable Devices

Employees may do business only on the following personal devices; a device that does not appear on this list may not be used for work nor may it connect to the Company's network:

- Apple iPhones and iPads

- Android smart phones and tablets

- BlackBerry smart phones and playbooks

Employees must maintain the original operating systems on their devices; for example, they may not use personal devices that have been "rooted" or "jailbroken."

How Employees Will Use BYOD

There are a number of options for employee use of BYOD, with varying levels of security risk for your company. The best choice for your company will depend on a number of factors, including the type of work employees do remotely, your company's security needs and comfort with risk, and whether your employees are willing to give up at least some of their privacy in exchange for the convenience of using their own device for work.

Your options here will also depend on the type of software solution you choose to help you manage BYOD. For example, if your employees really want and need access to confidential corporate documents from their mobile devices and can handle the loss of privacy, an MDM system that gives your company total control over the employee's device, just like it would have over a traditional corporate BlackBerry, would make sense. If your employees feel strongly about the privacy of their personal information, you might limit them to accessing only business email and calendaring functions from their mobile devices, using an MAM system to control those applications and the data associated with them.

Ultimately, you'll have to come up with your own policy language here, after deciding how you will allow employees to use BYOD and how your company will manage the security challenges. Here are a couple of examples:

Optional Language: Email Only

> Employees may use their personal devices solely to access their corporate email accounts. No Company data may be stored or downloaded to your personal computing device.

Optional Language: Corporate Documents

> Employees may use their personal devices to access their corporate email accounts and certain Company databases, depending on your position and job requirements. Any Company documents on an employee's personal mobile device must be encrypted and password-protected. Such documents must be securely deleted as soon as you are finished using them.

Privacy Concerns

If you issue company equipment to an employee, such as a computer or cell phone, your company owns that property. It may inspect or take back the property when it wishes, monitor the employee's use of the property, and so on. When an employee uses a personal device for work, however, the lines are less clear. On the one hand, employees are likely to feel that their vacation photos, personal contact lists, and personal online activities are private. On the other, your company still has some interest in what the employee does with the device and the company data it holds.

How you handle this issue depends, in part, on the type of mobile device or application management software your company will use. For example, some programs have become fairly sophisticated at separating business data from personal data, so that the company can control—and if necessary, remotely wipe—its information without endangering employees' photos, downloads, and other personal items. In these programs, business data is typically segregated into one area, which can then be managed and erased.

No matter what type of system you use, you run a risk of accessing and even destroying private information. Employees must know that this risk is one of the costs of using their own device for work.

Your Personal Information

When you use a personal computing device for work, the Company may have the ability to access and review information stored on the device. The Company may also need to remotely wipe the device in case it is lost, stolen, or otherwise subject to a security breach. In this case, some or all of your personal information may be lost. You should not expect that any files, records, or other data stored on a personal device you use for work will be private.

Don't Use Daddy's Phone

The CEO of Mimecast—who played a role in developing his company's BYOD policy—fell victim to it while on vacation. He had used his BYOD smartphone to take photos of the family's trip to South Africa. However, all of those photos were remotely wiped, per company policy, when his five-year-old daughter entered the wrong password five times in a row. The company had considered a "partial wipe" policy, but ultimately decided it did not provide enough security for company information. The company surveyed 500 IT professionals and found that 21% believed BYOD had been a risk to their businesses; for 26% more, that risk was great enough to deny employees the right to use BYOD altogether.

Security of Personal Devices

Security concerns are greatly heightened when employees use their own personal devices for work. If your company issues smart phones or other devices, it can control what's on the device, what it can do, and all security features. With a personal device, you must rely on the employees themselves to implement certain security safeguards. The sample policy language below adopts a number of common security rules; you will need to adapt your policy to reflect the requirements and operation of the software solution you choose.

Security of Personal Mobile Devices

Although using personal mobile devices is convenient and efficient for employees, it can also pose a risk to the security of the Company's proprietary information. If these devices are lost, stolen, or hacked into, an outsider could get access the Company's network or data.

To prevent theft and loss of data, employees who use their personal mobile devices for work must follow these guidelines:

Before using a personal mobile device to connect to the Company's network or otherwise do business, employees must submit their personal device to the IT department, which will register the device and configure it with the necessary applications and tools. Employees must maintain any Company applications loaded onto their personal devices.

All personal computing devices used for work must be password-protected. [Provide additional guidance on your Company's password policy here, such as "Passwords will expire every two months, and you may not choose a password you have used in the past. The device must automatically lock after ten failed login attempts."]

Use the same malware precautions when using a personal device for business as are required for Company computers. You must keep your anti-virus software up to date and use it. Don't open attachments or files without scanning for viruses.

Employees are responsible for the security of the personal devices they use for business. Keep the device with you whenever possible. Always log or sign off before leaving a personal device unattended. Do not allow others to use a personal device you use for work.

Employees must immediately notify the Company's IT department if their personal computing device is lost or stolen, so the Company may remotely lock or wipe the device.

Reimbursing Employees

Your policy should also address whether and how your company will reimburse employees who use their personal mobile devices for work. There are a number of options here, from a flat monthly stipend to an expense reimbursement model. No matter which option you choose, however, you should make sure that employees are being fully compensated for their work-related expenses. Some states require employers to pay for all tools, equipment, and other items employees need to perform their jobs. In these states, your company could face legal challenges if its BYOD program doesn't fully cover employee costs.

BYOD Can Increase Costs

One of the primary reasons employers switch to a BYOD model is to save money. But the math doesn't always work out. According to a 2012 survey by Xigo, 67% of companies that had adopted a BYOD plan hadn't seen any change in expenses, and 24% actually saw their costs go up. That leaves a measly 9% that has cut costs by moving to a BYOD model.

If you have decided not to reimburse employees for BYOD (after making sure this is legal in your state), you don't have to say anything in your policy. If you decide to reimburse employees, you'll need to survey employees on what they pay for their phone and data plans, how much (and in what ways) they will use their devices for work, and so on. Most commonly, employers who reimburse employees do so either with a set stipend payment or a percentage expense payment. Below are examples of how you might describe each plan.

Optional Language: Stipend Payment

Reimbursement for Use of Your Personal Device

Employees who use their personal mobile devices for work will be paid a set amount each month for work-related communications. The amount depends on how you use your device:

Phone only: Employees who use their devices only for telephone calls (or whose phones don't have a data plan and/or can't receive emails) will receive _____ per month.

Smart phone: Employees who use their devices for phone calls, texts, emails, and other work-related communications will receive _____ per month.

The Company anticipates that the above amounts will be sufficient to cover all work-related communication needs. If you believe you are not being fully reimbursed for all business use of your device, please speak to your manager.

Optional Language: Percentage Reimbursement

Reimbursement for Use of Your Personal Device

Employees who wish to use their personal mobile devices for work will be reimbursed a percentage of their monthly costs each month. Employees are responsible for paying the full cost of [*list services and fees you won't pay, such as "roaming charges, personal applications, and fees for exceeding the usage limit on your plan."*]

Employees must submit their bills each month for reimbursement. Employees may be reimbursed _____% of their costs, up to a limit of _____ per month.

Driving Safety

As is true of company-issued devices, employees should not use their own devices while driving. (Chapter 8 covers the use of cell phones, whether owned by the employee or the company, while driving.)

No Texting While Driving

Employees are prohibited from using any personal mobile device, such as a smart phone, or tablet, for work while driving. We are concerned for your safety and for the safety of other drivers and pedestrians, and texting, checking messages, going online, or otherwise using a mobile device while driving can lead to accidents.

If you must send or read a work-related message while driving, you must wait until you can pull over safety and stop the car before doing so.

Wage and Hour Concerns

Even more than for company-issued devices, personal devices make it way too easy for employee work overtime without the company knowing about it.

Overtime and Personal Mobile Devices

Our Company's overtime rules apply to any type of work done after hours, including using a personal mobile device for work. If you are eligible to earn overtime, all overtime work—including work done on your own device—must be approved in writing, in advance. Working overtime without permission violates Company policy and may result in disciplinary action.

> ! CAUTION
> **Don't forget the acknowledgment form.** If your company
> adopts the portable computing device policy covered in this chapter, make
> sure you require employees to sign an acknowledgment form. You'll find
> a sample acknowledgment form and instructions online at this book's
> companion page on Nolo's website; see the appendix for more information.

Putting It All Together: Sample Portable Computing Device Policy

Here's a sample portable computing device policy adopted by a manufacturing company. Although a handful of company executives need business phones when they travel and to connect with the company's servers remotely, the vast majority of company employees do not need mobile devices to do their jobs. After much thought, the company decides to forego BYOD for now, and instead purchase corporate BlackBerrys for the executive team.

Portable Computing Device Policy

Personal Use of Company-Issued Portable Computing Devices

The Company may provide you with a portable computing device (such as a smartphone or tablet). The Company may also permit you to access its network using a portable computing device to perform your job.

The Company's portable computing devices and network are intended for business use. You may use such computing devices for occasional personal purposes, but you may do so during nonwork hours only. You must also ensure that your personal use of the Company's portable computing devices does not interfere in any way with your job duties or performance. Any employee who abuses this privilege may be subject to discipline, up to and including termination.

If an employee's use of a Company-issued portable computing device results in fees or costs beyond what the Company would otherwise have to pay for the service, the employee will be required to reimburse the Company.

Use of Portable Computing Devices Is Not Private

The Company has the ability to access and review all information stored on the Company's portable computing devices and network. The Company reserves the right to perform such an inspection at any time, for any reason. You should not expect that any files, records, or other data stored on the Company's equipment and network will be private, even if you attempt to protect its privacy (for example, by using a password or designating it as "personal").

Content Rules for Portable Computing Devices

All of our policies and rules of conduct apply to employee use of Company-issued portable computing devices. All communications (email, instant messaging, and Internet access) on Company-issued portable computing devices are subject to the Company's policies on appropriate use. This means, for example, that employees may not send harassing messages, access pornographic or gambling websites, or violate any of the Company's other rules on appropriate communications content.

Security of Company-Issued Portable Computing Devices

Although portable computing equipment (such as laptops, tablets, personal digital assistants, or smartphones) can greatly improve our communications and efficiency, they can also pose a risk to the security of the Company's proprietary information. If these devices are lost, stolen, or hacked into, an outsider could have access to Company data or the Company's network.

To prevent theft and loss of data, employees who receive Company-issued portable computing equipment must follow these guidelines:

Employees should not download confidential Company information to a portable computing device unless it is absolutely necessary. If confidential Company information is stored on a portable computing device, you must delete that information securely as soon as you are finished using it. If you are not certain whether particular data qualifies as confidential Company information, ask your supervisor for assistance.

All data and files kept on a portable computing device must be encrypted, using Company-approved encryption software.

All Company-issued portable computing devices will require power-on passwords, which must be changed every two months. You must always log or sign off before leaving a portable computing device unattended.

If your Company-issued portable computing device is equipped with antivirus software, you must download or install updates to this software when instructed by the Company.

You may not download, install, or use any software programs on a Company-issued portable computing device unless that program has been approved by the IT department.

Use the same malware precautions when using a portable computing device as are required for Company computers. Do not open attachments to email or instant messages if you do not know the sender or otherwise aren't sure that the attachment is legitimate. Do not open, read, or download any file from the Internet without scanning it for viruses.

Employees are responsible for the security of portable computing devices issued to them. Keep portable computing devices in your possession whenever possible. If you must leave a portable computing device unattended, you must store it out of sight in a secure location, such as a hotel safe or locked filing cabinet at home. Never leave a portable computing device in a vehicle.

Employees must immediately notify the Company's IT department if their portable computing device is lost or stolen, so the Company may remotely delete all data stored on the device.

Don't Use Personal Mobile Devices for Work

We understand that employees may occasionally wish to use their own mobile devices—such as smartphones or tablets—for work. However, storing Company information on a personal mobile device or using such a device to access the Company's network creates unacceptable security risks. Therefore, employees are prohibited from using their own mobile devices for business purposes or from storing Company information on a personal mobile device. If you feel that you need a mobile device to do your job, please talk to your manager to find out whether you are eligible for a Company-issued device.

No Texting While Driving

Employees are prohibited from using any portable computing device for work-related matters while driving. We are concerned for your safety and for the safety of other drivers and pedestrians, and texting, checking messages, going online, or otherwise using a portable computing device while driving can lead to accidents.

If you must send or read a work-related message while driving, you must wait until you can pull over safely and stop the car before doing so.

Overtime and Portable Computing Devices

Our Company's overtime rules apply to any type of work done after hours, including using a Company-issued portable computing device (laptop, PDA, or smartphone, etc.) for work. All overtime work—including work done on a personal computing device—must be approved in writing, in advance. Working overtime without permission violates Company policy and may result in disciplinary action.

Cameras and Camera Phones

In This Chapter:

Policy Provisions for Cameras and Camera Phones

☐ Alternative 1: Banning Camera Phones and Other Recording Devices

☐ Alternative 2: Use Restrictions

    ☐ Prohibiting Cameras in Certain Areas

    ☐ Prohibiting Use of Cameras

    ☐ Guidelines for Camera Use

Phones are not the only digital devices that incorporate cameras: You can also find cameras on PDAs (personal digital assistants), MP3 players, and even binoculars. But camera phones are certainly the most prevalent and, as a result, have brought us many images we might never have seen otherwise, captured by people who just happened to have their phones with them. These images have exposed scandals, captured natural disasters, and caught celebrities in compromising positions. They've given rise to the "citizen journalist," ready to provide evidence of breaking events as they happen.

You Can Thank the Camera Phone

Don't believe that camera phones have already had a major impact on the way we see the world? Consider these images, all captured on camera phone:
- the execution of Saddam Hussein
- the London tube bombing
- protests in Myanmar by Buddhist monks
- the Asian tsunami
- the shootings at Virginia Tech, and
- some of the images of prisoner abuse from Abu Ghraib.

Of course, not all of the famous photos taken with camera phones are this weighty. You can also toss into the pile a picture of French soccer star Zinedine Zidane smoking a cigarette, after having starred in an antismoking campaign; pictures of Prince Harry dressed as a Nazi for a costume party; and the video of Michael Richards (who played Kramer on "Seinfeld") going off on a racist rant in a Los Angeles nightclub.

The very features that make camera phones so cool—their small size, portability, and dual function, which allow users to take photos on the sly—also make them a very real workplace danger. Employers have become increasingly worried about employees violating their coworkers' privacy by photographing them surreptitiously at work. Employers that have trade secrets to protect—whether in the form of documents, devices, processes, or personnel—are also understandably afraid that employees might use a camera phone to capture and transmit confidential information.

Camera phones pose a special risk to employers because a user can snap pictures without appearing to do so. And like digital cameras, camera phones allow users to download photos to their computers.

Whether your company's resident photographer is capturing dirty dancing at the company's holiday party or trade secrets on the factory floor ("Let's take a group photo … in front of the dye mixer!"), a camera or camera phone makes it possible for images and information to leave your company in a snap. This chapter explains your policy options for dealing with cameras and camera phones in the workplace. Alternative 1 is an outright ban on cameras and camera phones at work; Alternative 2 allows employees to bring their cameras and camera phones to work, but provides some restrictions on how and where employees may use them.

Alternative 1: Banning Cameras

The first decision you'll have to make is whether your company should prohibit photographic devices—cameras, video cameras, and camera phones—outright. Note that banning cameras is different from limiting their use, described below in "Alternative 2: Use Restrictions." A ban means employees may not bring cameras to the workplace, period.

Camera Bans: More Common Than You Might Think

Banning all cameras (and camera phones) in the workplace may seem like an extreme reaction to a somewhat theoretical problem—and, for some companies, that's exactly what it is. But the problems associated with secretly recording others are very real, especially in situations where privacy is at a premium. For example, many fitness clubs, gyms, and swimming pools have banned cameras and camera phones after naked locker room photos began circulating on the Internet. Certain night clubs and other hot spots where celebrities like to mingle ban camera phones. Some hospitals and courthouses also ban camera phones, as do many companies (including camera phone manufacturers, like Samsung and LG).

This is a very restrictive policy choice, suitable only for certain employers. A camera ban may be appropriate if:
- your company works on matters related to national security
- your company has strong confidentiality concerns or valuable trade secrets that can be photographed—for example, machinery, processes, or secret construction, or
- your business provides opportunities for personal privacy violations—for example, employees shower on site after handling hazardous materials.

Because so many cell phones come with a camera feature, an outright ban will pose a real hardship for employees. That's why you'll need to include an exception clause, giving employees who need their personal phones at work a way to get permission to have them.

No Camera Phones and Other Recording Devices

The use of cameras, video and audio recording devices, or digital devices (such as cell phones, MP3 players, or PDAs) that have recording capability can cause violations of privacy and breaches of confidentiality.

For that reason, we do not allow cameras, video or audio recording equipment, or cell phones or other digital devices that have these capabilities, on Company property. If you have such a device with you, you may either leave it in your car or [*provide another option, such as "with the receptionist" or "with the office manager"*].

If you believe that your personal circumstances require you to have your cell phone at work, and your cell phone has a camera or other recording capability, please talk to your supervisor.

Gadgets Without Cameras = Big Corporate Sales Opportunities

After a couple of years when it was almost impossible to find a cell phone without a camera, manufacturers of cell phones and other hand-held devices have started realizing that there's a large potential market for camera-free gadgets. In 2007, for example, Research in Motion released the BlackBerry 8800, a model intended especially for corporate and business use. The 8800 has no camera, at the urging of corporate customers concerned about security. Mike Lazaridis, the company's president, said, "There's a very strong demand out there for BlackBerrys without a camera. Not having one, that's a feature."

Ian Austen, "Can Executives Find Happiness With a Blackberry Without Its Scroll Wheel?," *The New York Times*, February 13, 2007.

Alternative 2: Use Restrictions

Many companies won't need to ban cameras outright. Instead, you might want to prohibit employees from bringing them into certain areas, prohibit employees from using the camera feature at work, and/or set some guidelines for taking photos at work.

Prohibiting Cameras in Certain Areas

Most companies can use this policy language, at least for restrooms. Adapt the policy to your workplace by including all areas where cameras could pose a security or privacy risk.

Restrictions on Camera Phones and Other Recording Devices

Employees may not bring cameras, video and audio recording devices, or digital devices (such as cell phones, MP3 players, or PDAs) that have recording capability, to any of the following areas: restrooms, [*other private or secure areas, such as "locker rooms," "changing rooms," "lab," "R & D," "shop floor," and so on*].

Lessons From the Real World

It's a bird! It's a plane! It's a plane photographing our trade secrets!
In March 1969, employees at DuPont's plant in Beaumont, Texas, noticed a plane circling overhead. DuPont later discovered that the plane held Rolfe and Gary Christopher, who had been hired to photograph new construction at the plant. The Christophers refused

to tell DuPont's investigators who had hired them or what they planned to do with the photographs.

DuPont sued the Christophers, claiming they had stolen the company's trade secrets and sold them. DuPont claimed that the photographs depicted an area where DuPont planned to begin producing methanol using a confidential, unpatented process. Because the plant was under construction when the photographs were taken, parts of the process were visible from the air—and DuPont claimed that someone could use this information to piece together its top-secret procedures.

The Christophers argued that they couldn't be sued for trade secret theft because they hadn't violated any laws or any duty to DuPont. They were in public airspace when they took the pictures. Because they didn't work for DuPont, they had no legal obligation to protect its trade secrets. In short, the Christophers argued that they had gotten hold of the photos fair and square, even if they did reveal DuPont's methanol process.

The Court ruled in favor of DuPont, finding that the Christophers had taken its trade secret by "improper means." Had the Christophers or their unnamed client used reverse engineering or independent research to figure out DuPont's process, that would have been fine. But taking it from DuPont without permission, at a time when DuPont was taking precautions to keep the secret, was not.

E.I. DuPont DeNemours & Co. v. Christopher, 431 F.2d 1012 (5th Cir. 1970).

Prohibiting Use of Cameras

Some companies choose to allow employees to bring their camera phones to work, but prohibit use of their recording capabilities. This approach makes sense for many companies, particularly if many employees have camera phones and an outright ban would be met with strong resistance. If your company has privacy and trade secret concerns, you can combine this language with the language above that bans cameras in certain areas, such as restrooms and laboratories.

This type of policy will be difficult to enforce; it can be tough to tell whether someone is actually taking a picture with a camera phone. It will work only if your company has a relatively high level of trust in its employees.

No Use of Camera Phones and Other Recording Devices at Work

Employees may not use any cameras, video and audio recording devices, or video or recording features of cell phones, MP3 players, PDAs, or other digital devices that contain such capability, at work.

Street Harassment Victims Fight Back—With Camera Phones

First came the camera phone, then the camera-phone voyeur, then the camera-phone crime fighter. You may have heard about "upskirt" photos—or their close relative, "downblouse" photos—taken with camera phones. Typically, these photos are taken surreptitiously. So why have we heard of them? Because there are entire websites devoted to them, where amateur voyeurs can post their photos.

Now, the public harassment tables have turned, with the advent of the antiharassment website. These sites, like Holla Back New York (http://hollabacknyc.blogspot.com), allow readers to post camera phone photos of people who have harassed them in public, along with a narrative of exactly what happened. The blog's motto: If you can't slap 'em, snap 'em.

Guidelines for Camera Use

Your company may wish to allow employees to use their cameras or camera phones, either in areas where your policy doesn't prohibit such use or only in some situations—for example, at company events or to capture candid photos for a company newsletter. If so, it's a good idea to provide guidelines for taking and using pictures, especially of other employees. This will help you protect employee privacy.

Guidelines for Camera Use

Employees who use cameras, camera phones, or other digital devices to capture photos or video on Company property or at Company events must follow these rules:

1. Employees may take pictures of other employees, customers, clients, or visitors only with their permission. If you intend to publicize the pictures—for example, by posting them on the Internet, using them in a Company newsletter, or submitting them to a photography contest—you must disclose this to the people whose picture you are taking. If, after taking the pictures, you decide to publicize them in some way, you must obtain permission to do so from the people who appear in them.

2. Employees may not take pictures of Company trade secrets or other confidential information. This includes, but is not limited to, [*list the most common types of trade secrets your company has, such as "customer lists," "pricing information," "recipes," "design plans," "software code," and so on*].

3. Employees may not take or use pictures to harass, embarrass, or annoy others. All Company policies—including the Company's policies on harassment, discrimination, and professional conduct—apply to workplace photographs.

> 4. If you have any questions about whether it's appropriate to take a photograph at work or use a workplace photograph in a particular way, please ask your supervisor.

CAUTION

Don't forget the acknowledgment form. If your company adopts the camera phone policy covered in this chapter, make sure you require employees to sign an acknowledgment form. You'll find a sample acknowledgment form and instructions online at this book's companion page at Nolo's website; see the appendix for more information.

Putting It All Together: Sample Camera Phone Policy

Here's a sample camera phone policy adopted by a (fictional) company that manufactures packaging material. Many employees have cell phones with a camera feature, so the company doesn't want to ban camera phones outright. Also, employees often use their camera phones to take pictures of company parties and employee gatherings for the company's newsletter. But the company is also concerned about employee privacy: Employees change into protective gear at work. And the company wants to keep its manufacturing process confidential. The company decides to prohibit employees from bringing cameras and camera phones into certain areas, and to adopt guidelines for use of cameras at work.

Camera Phone Policy

Restrictions on Camera Phones and Other Recording Devices

Employees may not bring cameras, video and audio recording devices, or digital devices (such as cell phones, MP3 players, or PDAs) that have recording capability, to any of the following areas: restrooms, locker rooms, the research and development department, and Areas A through D of the plant facility.

Guidelines for Camera Use

Employees who use cameras, camera phones, or other digital devices to capture photos or video on Company property or at Company events must follow these rules:

1. Employees may take pictures of other employees, customers, clients, or visitors only with their permission. If you intend to publicize the pictures—for example, by posting them on the Internet, using them in a Company newsletter, or submitting them to a photography contest—you must disclose this to the people whose picture you are taking. If, after taking the pictures, you decide to publicize them in some way, you must obtain permission to do so from the people who appear in them.

2. Employees may not take pictures of Company trade secrets or other confidential information. This includes, but is not limited to, the manufacturing line and equipment, specifications for Company products, memos and notes from meetings regarding Company products, all information about products in development, customer lists, and any documents or photographs that have been marked "Confidential: For Internal Use Only."

3. Employees may not take or use pictures to harass, embarrass, or annoy others. All Company policies—including the Company's policies on harassment, discrimination, and professional conduct—apply to workplace photographs.

4. If you have any questions about whether it's appropriate to take a photograph at work or use a workplace photograph in a particular way, please ask your supervisor.

Using the Interactive Forms

This book comes with interactive files that you can access online at **www.nolo.com/back-of-book/TECH.html**. To use the files, your computer must have specific software programs installed. The files in this book are provided as RTFs. You can open, edit, print, and save these form files with most word processing programs such as Microsoft Word, Windows WordPad, and recent versions of WordPerfect.

> **TIP**
>
> **Note to Macintosh users.** These forms were designed for use with Windows. They should also work on Macintosh computers; however Nolo cannot provide technical support for non-Windows users.

Editing RTFs

Here are some general instructions about editing RTF forms in your word processing program. Refer to the book's instructions and sample agreements for help about what should go in each blank.

- **Underlines.** Underlines indicate where to enter information. After filling in the needed text, delete the underline. In most word processing programs you can do this by highlighting the underlined portion and typing CTRL-U.
- **Bracketed and italicized text.** Bracketed and italicized text indicates instructions. Be sure to remove all instructional text before you finalize your document.
- **Alternative text.** Alternative text gives you the choice between two or more text options. Delete those options you don't want to use. Renumber numbered items, if necessary.
- **Signature lines.** Signature lines should appear on a page with at least some text from the document itself.

Every word processing program uses different commands to open, format, save, and print documents, so refer to your software's help documents for help using your program. Nolo cannot provide technical support for questions about how to use your computer or your software.

CAUTION

In accordance with U.S. copyright laws, the forms and audio files provided by this book are for your personal use only.

List of Forms

Form Title	File Name
Computer and Software Use Policy	Software.rtf
Email Policy	Email.rtf
Internet Policy	Internet.rtf
Instant Messaging Policy	IM.rtf
Blogs and Personal Posting Policy	Blogs.rtf
Cell Phone Policy	Cell.rtf
Portable Computing Device Policy	PortableComputingDevice.rtf
Camera Phone Policy	CameraPhone.rtf
Electronic Communications and Equipment Policy Acknowledgment Form	Acknowledgment.rtf
Company-Sponsored Social Media Policy	SocialMedia.rtf

Index

C

 Go to Nolo.com/newsletters to sign up for free newsletters and discounts on Nolo products.

- **Nolo's Special Offer.** A monthly newsletter with the biggest Nolo discounts around.

- **Landlord's Quarterly.** Deals and free tips for landlords and property managers.

 Don't forget to check for updates. Find this book at **Nolo.com** and click "Legal Updates."

Let Us Hear From You

 Register your Nolo product and give us your feedback at Nolo.com/customer-support/ productregistration.

- Once you've registered, you qualify for technical support if you have any trouble with a download (though most folks don't).

- We'll send you a coupon for 15% off your next Nolo.com order!

TECH3

⚖ NOLO *and* USA TODAY

Cutting-Edge Content, Unparalleled Expertise

The Busy Family's Guide to Money
by Sandra Block, Kathy Chu & John Waggoner • $19.99

The Work From Home Handbook
Flex Your Time, Improve Your Life
by Diana Fitzpatrick & Stephen Fishman • $19.99

Retire Happy
What You Can Do NOW to Guarantee a Great Retirement
by Richard Stim & Ralph Warner • $19.99

The Essential Guide for First-Time Homeowners
Maximize Your Investment & Enjoy Your New Home
by Ilona Bray & Alayna Schroeder • $19.99

Easy Ways to Lower Your Taxes
Simple Strategies Every Taxpayer Should Know
by Sandra Block & Stephen Fishman • $19.99

First-Time Landlord
Your Guide to Renting Out a Single-Family Home
by Attorney Janet Portman, Marcia Stewart & Michael Molinski • $19.99

Stopping Identity Theft
10 Easy Steps to Security
by Scott Mitic, CEO, TrustedID, Inc. • $19.99

The Mom's Guide to Wills & Estate Planning
by Attorney Liza Hanks • $21.99

Running a Side Business
How to Create a Second Income
by Attorneys Richard Stim & Lisa Guerin • $21.99

Nannies and Au Pairs
Hiring In-Home Child Care
by Ilona Bray, J.D. • $19.99

The Judge Who Hated Red Nail Polish
& Other Crazy But True Stories of Law and Lawyers
by Ilona Bray, Richard Stim & the Editors of Nolo • $19.99

ORDER DIRECTLY FROM NOLO.COM AND SAVE!

Prices subject to change.

⚖ NOLO *Online Legal Forms*

Nolo offers a large library of legal solutions and forms, created by Nolo's in-house legal staff. These reliable documents can be prepared in minutes.

Create a Document

- **Incorporation.** Incorporate your business in any state.
- **LLC Formations.** Gain asset protection and pass-through tax status in any state.
- **Wills.** Nolo has helped people make over 2 million wills. Is it time to make or revise yours?
- **Living Trust (avoid probate).** Plan now to save your family the cost, delays, and hassle of probate.
- **Trademark.** Protect the name of your business or product.
- **Provisional Patent.** Preserve your rights under patent law and claim "patent pending" status.

Download a Legal Form

Nolo.com has hundreds of top quality legal forms available for download—bills of sale, promissory notes, nondisclosure agreements, LLC operating agreements, corporate minutes, commercial lease and sublease, motor vehicle bill of sale, consignment agreements and many more.

Review Your Documents

Many lawyers in Nolo's consumer-friendly lawyer directory will review Nolo documents for a very reasonable fee. Check their detailed profiles at **Nolo.com/lawyers**.

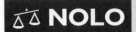

⚖ NOLO *Lawyer Directory*

Find an Attorney

Qualified lawyers · In-depth profiles

When you want help with a serious legal problem, you don't want just any lawyer—you want an expert in the field who can give you and your family up-to-the-minute advice. You need a lawyer who has the experience and knowledge to answer your questions about personal injury, wills, family law, child custody, drafting a patent application or any other specialized legal area you are concerned with.

Nolo's Lawyer Directory is unique because it provides an extensive profile of every lawyer. You'll learn about not only each lawyer's education, professional history, legal specialties, credentials and fees, but also about their philosophy of practicing law and how they like to work with clients.

www.nolo.com